MW01074156

# Understanding Children's Emotions

filliozat.net

© Isabelle Filliozat, 2013

Isabelle Filliozat

# Understanding
# Children's Emotions

Heart to heart parenting
-raising your child's EQ

Translated from the French by Jane Martin

Original title, *Au cœur des émotions de l'enfant*
First published by J.C.Lattès en 1999

*To my father,*
*Who was, and still is, a militant protesting against the use of the word 'education', prefering to 'accompany' his children through life. Harshly marked to this day by the violence he received from his own parents, he didn't always succeed in being with his own children, but was certainly there for them. He loved and respected me, always considered me as a person and was able to give me what he hadn't received.*

*To Margot and Adrian,*
*Who made me a mother.*

*To Suos Pom, midwife and Pr. Biziau and Corinne Drescher-Zaninger, obstetricians, who all accompanied me through the most intense moments of happiness in my life.*

*To LLL Leche League and its President Claude Didier-jean-Jouveau, who were there to help me breastfeed my children and open up a whole dimension of wonderful intimacy for me.*

## Acknowledgements

*I would like to thank all the people who contributed to this book, all those who inspired me, asked me questions and obliged me to think things over, all the parents who allowed me to be a witness to their their lives and all the children who confided in me. The examples are drawn from my professional activity and personal life or that of my friends.*

*I would like to thank Marianne Leconte who believed in me and helped me, more than she could ever imagine, to both foster and improve my writing talents.*

*I would like to thank Patrice Le Bon for his support, his trust, and for being so exacting.*

*I would like to thank Jean Bernard, Adrian and Margot Fried for their love.*

*You say,*
*Dealings with children are tiresome.*
*You're right.*
*You say,*
*- Because we have to lower ourselves to their intellect.*
*- Lower, stoop, bend, crouch down.*
*You are mistaken.*
*It isn't that which is so tiring.*
*But because we have to reach up to their feelings.*
*Reach up, stretch, stand on our tiptoes.*
*As not to offend.*

—*Janusz Korczak*

*When I am Little Again and The Child's Right to Respect.* (English translation by E.P. Kulawiec of original Polish works published in 1925 and 1929; Lanham, Maryland, University Press of America.

# Introduction

Having a knowing heart means knowing how to understand and love other people, how to find fulfilment, be oneself at all moments and react with emotional intelligence in difficult circumstances: conflict, failure, mourning, separation and all the trials and tribulations of life. It even includes coping with success in its various forms or simply enjoying being with people. It's the ability to tune into happiness, overcome difficulty, choose the right way of life and enjoy happy relationships. Who wouldn't want that for their children?

What is it that holds us back and prevents us finding happiness? What is it that maims our hearts? It can all be traced back to childhood suffering (often unconscious) and consequent fears: fear of being judged, wounded, humiliated, rejected or ignored, fear of failure that makes us doubt our ability to achieve, fear of being unable to find our place among others, fear of others and fear of dying... Since this is a question of fear, suffering and unexpressed anger, not of any constitutional flaw or mental quirk that prevents people from being open to themselves and to others, we can help our children by avoiding hurtful behavior but rather instilling trust and confidence.

Present day society is not like that of the past. Advice on upbringing that dates from times gone by is no longer appropriate. Nowadays, the pathway to success depends on self-confidence, self-reliance and ability to relate. Tomorrow it will be even more so. Ease of communication and emotional control have become at least as important as technical skills. A knowing heart, in both the personal and professional worlds, has become an even more fundamental asset. Taking care of our children's intelligence quotient (IQ) is not sufficient. We must take care of their emotional quotient (EQ). Moreover, numerous learning difficulties originate in some form of emotional blockage.

No parent likes to see his child sprawled in front of the television or plugged into a computer game. How can we help our children resist screen contagion of whatever type? How can we help them resist the violence and hypnotic rhythm of the images in electronic games, clips, ads, films, popular programs and even cartoons?

No parent can stand the idea of his child sinking into delinquency, drink or drugs. How can we arm our children against such temptations when violent behavior is present in the playground and when alcohol and drugs come earlier and earlier into our children's lives?

No parent wants his child to get caught up in a sect as a blind follower who has abdicated his own willpower in favour of someone else's. How can we instill enough confidence in our children and enough inner security and autonomy to prevent them succumbing to the seduction of some guru?

Violent behavior and unhealthy dependency on people, television, drugs or medecine all indicate attempts to keep uncontrollable emotions at bay. These symptoms are rooted in early childhood, covering relational deficiency, deep hurt or communication breakdown.

Shyness, feelings of unworthiness or, on the contrary, overconfidence are all traits of character that have a story to tell. Hurt feelings, misunderstood intentions, hasty judgements... There are so many painful possibilities in the parent-child relationship.

A child is a person. Emotions are heartfelt core-feelings and the expression of a child's life deep-down. Knowing how to listen to and respect this means knowing how to listen to and respect him or her as an individual. Parents are so often destabilized by the intensity of their children's feelings that they automatically try to calm them down, stop the tears and cut off the emotional overflow. Nonetheless, every emotion carries a meaning, an intention, and is destined to heal. Emotional discharge is the way of freeing oneself from the consequences of a painful experience and the repression of these necessary emotions is harmful. It forces us to invent all sorts of defense mechanisms, including distressful repetition, compulsive behavior and physical symptoms ranging from *tension* and *discomfort* to *serious illness*.

The time has come to avoid becoming a slave to our emotions by learning how to identify, name, understand and use them. It is necessary to ensure the welfare of our children and the adults they will grow into.

We now know that the formative years are before the age of six. So, what should we do, or not do? And how? And most of all, how should we live our lives? All (responsible) parents are asking themselves these questions and more.

Women are subjected to an onslaught of advice as soon as they show the first signs of pregnancy. Everybody airs their opinion about breastfeeding, sleep, how to rear a baby according to recipe and later, about limits, obedience and punishment, "You must be sure not to let them sleep in your bed." "You have to know where to draw the line." "A baby needs sleep." "A boy mustn't be allowed to play with doll." "You mustn't console them when they fall down or they'll be cry-babies." "If you let them do what they want, you'll make them into delinquents." "You must do this." "You mustn't do that." And this is just the first chapter of a whole series of musts and mustn'ts. All new parents are subjected to well-meant advice and questions which insinuate more than they ask about their educational principles and practice. One piece of advice will contradict another. In fact, there's loads of advice but precious little information. With each and every person having his own idea and voicing it emphatically, objective information is rarely offered. So many opinions are delivered with a degree of virulence matched only by their irrationality and absence of serious analysis. Young parents have a hard job sorting out the diverse concepts and are soon disorientated or completely bewildered. The advice is often sandwiched with more or less explicit threats, "You don't realize it, but that's how you get drug addicts, blame", "It comes from the mother's side" or explanations, "It's because the parents are divorcing."

Far from me to propose yet another book of such advice. Parents live their day-to-day life with their children, and know them better than any 'expert', whether pediatrician or psychoanalyst. However, sometimes misunderstandings and blockages can bias proper understanding and impair a harmonious relationship. If there's any need of an expert, it's just to remove the obstacles to understanding.

This book is to help you understand where the problem lies, avoid a difficulty when possible, sort out a complicated situation and get past some of the hurdles.

A new mother and father need guidelines rather than advice, and sufficient confidence to trust both themselves and their children.

Two fundamental concepts underpin the ideas in this book:
• Children inform us of their needs at each stage of their development, as long as we know how to listen to them and decode their particular language.
• Parents can understand their children and adopt the right attitude with them as long as they don't automatically follow the educational principles commonly dealt out, blindly subscribe to 'expert' opinions, let themselves be trapped in strict precepts issuing from their own, uncriticized education, or have not managed to heal the wounds received in their own lives.

Should we talk about our children's education without considering the one we received and how we have been marked by it, whether consciously or not? When situations or attitudes in our children annoy us or bring out our violence, we can be sure that we have something to heal in our own life in order to seize what's going on and be able to act fairly and efficiently, without the distortion of our own past history. When our relationships with our children are too difficult, it is more than likely that events in our own lives are at the bottom of it, and it would be wise to seek help from a psychotherapist.

Can we help our children develop their emotional quotient? How can we trust ourselves as parents? These questions are dealt with in the first chapter.

There is no infallible recipe concerning upbringing. Even if there are laws governing development that it can be useful to be familiar with, there are no musts, no miracle solutions for producing a 'successful' adult. What may be true at one moment may not be later on. Rather than searching for ready-made answers and infallible recipes, why not learn to think and decide for ourselves? In the second chapter, I propose seven questions you can ask yourselves to help you react more adequately in a whole range of situations.

The feeling of identity stems from self-awareness, that precious knowledge of our emotions. In chapter III we explore the world of emotions. Should we encourage our children to repress their feelings so as to be 'strong', or should we pay attention to their fears, tears and anger? How can we help them to develop courage without forfeiting their feelings?

In chapters IV, V, VI and VII, we explore the different dimensions of fear, anger, joy and sadness. When these emotions are not taken into account, a child may well retreat into a form of depression. We decode the symptoms in chapter VIII. Dramatic situations and ordeals are part of any child's life. In chapter IX, we envisage how to accompany death, separation, sickness in order to help our children get over these and other forms of suffering. In chapter X, we look at ideas about how to enhance pleasure and happiness in the children we love. Before embarking on a world tour of emotions, there's just one last reminder:

our children do not expect us to be perfect, just human. We can't help making mistakes. It's part of every learning process. So, we shall not bother about being a good mother or father, just to paying attention to our children's needs.

Certain passages in the book may surprise you, certain assertions may seem unusual… take the time to listen to how they echo in you. During conferences and courses so many people have come to me to say that there's nothing extraordinary about what I say, that it's perfectly obvious once you start looking at things from that angle!

When parents wonder about the consequences of their behavior on their children, they are often told they worry too much. They are being aggressed by those who have pre-established replies, without bothering about the emotional cost for their children. Who is the better parent? Asking questions is an essential part of human nature and serves us well. If you think you're doing everything the wrong way, don't be discouraged. You've bought this book, which means you're ready to learn how to better respect yourself and your children, to learn more about your and their emotions. These are pretty new notions, in fact.

Let's think back. Not so long ago, people were whipping children or leaving them in a dark cupboard, without anybody raising an eyebrow. Nobody had anything to say about threats, blows, indifference. The little monsters had to be broken in and taught how to behave. All sorts of corporal punishment were allowed, and children had no right to protest because it was all for their *good*, even when it made them feel bad. "Spare the rod and spoil the child" is a well-known saying! Only two or three generations ago, children had nothing but duties. All the rights were on the side of the parents (the *Declaration of the Rights of the Child* was adopted by UN General Assembly Resolution of 10 December 1959). We are improving on our parents and our children will improve on us. That's how things evolve.

If we feel guilty about an attitude towards our children, well, we may just look back on where we came from and at what we were submitted to as a child. Our guilt will do no good to our children. We have to assume the responsibility of this difficult role for which we are so ill-prepared. Being a parent is a really hard job (impossible according to Freud) since we are so painfully confronted with our own limits and unhealed wounds, not to mention the inevitable reproaches of our children. They need to question our ways in order to grow up, demarcate their way of being and then go on to lead their own lives.

If however we were tempted to accuse ourselves of being bad parents, we could just take a look at the sort of help and support we actually receive in that function. Are there enough grandparents, aunts, uncles, nannies, godparents and friends here to help? Looking after a baby means the sort of round-the-clock availability that is too much for one person. When the weight of responsibilty is on only one of the parents, especially when isolated, it's impossible to expect him or her to cope with the intense needs of an infant. There is no point in expecting too much of oneself. Being indulgent and, more than anything, expressing our own emotions and needs will make things be better for everybody.

Child rearing is less like a permanent battle when we know how to listen to our children, allow them to liberate their inner tensions, and offer the possibility of emotional discharge. Emotional intelligence restores love and connectedness for the whole family. Plus, the abilities children will learn will help them face all the difficulties they'll meet in their future life.

I hope you will find this book a ressource to help you live more happily in your family, for this is my intention in writing it.

# **Chapter I**

## Can we develop our children's EQ?

When I was pregnant with my first child, I made a wish that he or she would be good without being servile, have a will without being domineering, be brave and resourceful without being proud or cynical, find happiness both inwardly and with others.

It was my wish that my child might have a knowing heart.

# 1
# A Knowing Heart

A knowing heart is one able to solve the problems we meet during our lives, whether they are related to other people, personal trials, suffering, sickness or death. To weather such situations in the best way, we must be in possession of the inner wisdom to control fear, anger and sadness.

A knowing heart is able to bravely and wisely cope with everything human. It enables us to pacify difficult relationships and deal with everyday challenges. It leads us to constantly read meaning into life and evolve positively. It is what helps us to further our projects, find our way and attain self-achievement. Essential for all the mundane mishaps, it is doubly so for the painful earthquakes that can shake the very foundations of our existence.

Intelligence in relationships is of course rooted in emotional intelligence, but here I choose to separate the two. In another book I will treat the capacity to make and maintain bonds, to love and to separate, to understand others and to resolve conflicts. For the moment, I will concentrate on the idea of the emotional quotient.

Respecting children's emotions means allowing them to feel their own identity and become aware of themselves here and now. It's treating them as people not objects. It's giving them permission to be different from ourselves and respond in their very own way to the question, "Who am I?" It's also helping them to perceive today as different from yesterday or tomorrow, to be aware of their inner resources, strengths and weaknesses. It's giving them the knowledge that they're going somewhere, in *their own* way, on *their own* path through life.

Children mainly learn from their parents, whose educational attitude determines their degree of emotional intelligence. Children copy their parents and tend to follow examples far more readily than advice! Unconscious messages are as powerful as conscious words and deeds, if not more so. Helping our children develop their EQ obliges us to develop ours. Helping a child to grow up is a way of growing up ourselves. Our children are the mirrors of our inner reality, bring us up against our limits and teach us to love. They are excellent spiritual guides, if only we know how to listen to them.

Having a knowing heart means being able to love and gain substance through the ordeals we meet in life.

# 2
## Trusting our inner voice

Margot was about fourteen months old and often woke up in the night. Tired out, I went to consult a pediatrician professing a specialization in child psychiatry. After only a few minutes, she rather brutally announced: "So, that's the reason why!" My daughter, at the time, went to sleep while suckling and that, according to this lady doctor, was the at root of all our troubles. She had cast her verdict and it was up to me to accept it. She was not the slightest bit interested in me, my daughter or her father. Breastfeeding was the problem! Her logic was faultless: my daughter went to sleep on my breast, so when I put her to bed and she woke up to find the breast had disappeared, she would cry. The solution to the problem (according to her) was to take away the evening breastfeed so Margot could go to sleep 'on her own'. She would, of course cry, but would get used to it in three or four days at the most, and the tears would cease…

Oh Margot, I'm so sorry! How I regret having listened to that woman. I left you to cry. You cried for forty interminable minutes and then went to sleep in your father's arms. That first night, you woke up every two hours. Sadly, feeling guilty because of that doctor, I did it again the next day, and the day after. Four days later you cried just as much for your feed and of course, you slept even less well at night. So, I decided to ignore the specialist and

23

listen to you. I gave you what you wanted and what you needed: milk, closeness – a breastfeed. We installed your bed next to ours. You went to sleep happily and reassured, you slept better.

In fact, as I understood much later, after extensive reading and thanks to an intelligent psychoanalyst, you didn't have a sleeping problem at all. You just moved about between two sequences of deep sleep and, without actually waking, you sought your safety boundaries, your landmarks which were my smell and my breast. It's only if you couldn't feel me near you that you really woke up and cried. The pediatrician was, in fact quite right, you were looking for my breast. It's her solution that was all wrong. All I needed was to keep you near me at night in a bed next to mine!

Numerous parents take their little one into bed with them but don't dare admit it and often feel guilty about it. They've hitched onto the notion that it's 'not right' or may in some way or another, stop their children growing up as they should. In most countries round the world, the idea that children should sleep right through the night doesn't exist, and children sleep with their mothers as long as they're breastfeeding, until two or three years old. Some experts claim the the parents' bed is a place for a couple's intimacy. Why can't we be creative? A bed isn't the only place for love-making! Of course, children mustn't separate their parents, but a sleeping baby doesn't have that power. If the parents use this night-time sleeping partner to create a distance between them, then it's not the child's fault. If there is a refusal to make love with the pretext of the baby's presence, then another excuse would be found in his absence. The sexual desire for a child's body is harmful. The use of the baby's presence to push away the partner or reassure the mother is perverse and problematical, but not the mothering in itself.

A baby takes up a lot of room in a bed, so in order to happily accommodate everybody's needs, it's easy to bring a cot next to the parental bed, thus solving many a problem.

Isn't it a violence toward the baby to expect him to sleep without hearing his parents' breathing or smelling his mother? It sure serves adult peace and quiet (or our idea of peace and quiet), but the cost is high. Early separation does not lead to independence, but rather to fear of abandonment which has quite the reverse effect. Independence stems from a feeling of security. Maybe we should ask ourselves why the fear of abandonment is so prevalent, could it be related to this early separation habit? Fortunately, present-day books about bringing up children are getting past the taboo and are bringing new understanding and permission to parents. Many small children's books show baby bear cuddling up against mommy or daddy bear for the night.

Pediatricians do not always know better. Their analysis is no more than a theoretical standpoint. Our baby is not just an abstraction but a real, live being. If theories are to bring understanding, they must help us to better listen to our children rather than make them stay quiet and obedient. If a doctor, psychologist, some sort of expert or our mother-in-law tries to make us feel guilty, we should just leave. Only paying attention to what helps we may listen to our child. If I insist so much, it's because mothers are particularly vulnerable, especially with their first child, but also with the others since no child is the spitting image of another. Most mothers want to do things right and feel responsible for the life they have brought into the world.

It's so easy to feel inadequate when faced with the small child whose needs are they're there to satisfy. They have to cope with new responsibilities, a new job, trained only by the upbringing they themselves received. So they fall easy prey to people who like to give lessons of whatever sort. Bringing up children is a sore, sore subject, which fires extremes of conviction and vehemence. People argue right, left and centre about this, and families find it difficult to keep an even keel and avoid dissension and division.

It's so important to take into account both a mother's vulnerability and the intensity of such debates, taking care before the birth to choose helpful, positive people able to understand a mother's feelings towards her baby rather than deliver their personal ideology. When we blindly follow someone else's ideas, we can so easily make mistakes. We'll get a better answer in asking ourselves: "Does it says yes inside of me" or "Does it says no"? If we feel an intuitive 'yes', we do it. If it's 'no', we don't! We can listen to the wisdom of our heart, as long as we listen also to our child's heartfelt feelings. We can trust our child and listen to what his cries are trying to tell us, as well as his attitudes. His behavior gives the clues to what is distressing him. What he is unable to express with words he is expressing with symptoms. No need to panic, it's a form of language that he is speaking to us, his mother or father, and we can learn how to communicate. That doesn't mean that his language is necessarily easy to decode. Knowing that there is always a form of distress behind his cries or symptoms makes them tricky to fathom out. Distress can come from way back, whether in his own life or that of an ancestor. It often happens that a child will mirror part of the unconscious mind of his parents (or grandparents). In the case of persistent distress, it would be wise to consult a psychotherapist, whose role is to help us explore our inner self in order to find the origin of the difficulty and undo whatever emotional knots are affecting both us and our child's subconscious. He or she will listen and offer tools, but we are the one to find the answer. Better seek mediation, not advice. We don't need to accept peremptory opinions or hasty definitions. Someone else's convictions cannot help us. We will find solutions by connecting with our child, in whatever form of dialogue is possible, by feeling things out and trying things out. Each relationship is a unique creation.

# Chapter II

## Seven Questions To Ask Yourself To Know How To Respond In (Almost) All Situations

A journalist was interviewing Françoise Dolto: "Do you have problems bringing up your own children?"

She answered: "Yes, all children have difficulty understanding what's going on in the world because they interpret it in a magical way. Before (my children were) five, it was a daily task to understand what was going on in their child's mind[1]."

This famous lady and doctor gives us a precious lesson in humility! Françoise Dolto listened to, guided and helped thousands of children and parents. She had incredible intuition, profound wisdom and huge knowledge of the workings of the mind. And yet, she had more questions than answers when facing her own children. Each child is a unique individual and confronts us with his individuality.

To apply systematic recipes according to pre-determined educational rules is the outright denial of a person as a subject, however small he may be. To ask onself questions when faced with a child is proof of the desire to treat him individually.

But which questions?

# 1

# What's he experiencing?

A child is a person. He's graced with his own thoughts, emotions, fantasies and mental pictures.

Parents can feel at a loss when dealing with the hyper-sensitivity of a small child and the intensity of his affects. It often seems that a mere nothing (from the adult point of view) will tighten his little face and make him burst into tears. The slightest frustration can result in immense anger. A brain that hasn't yet matured cannot confer the mental requisites for emotional control. Young as he is, he doesn't know how to think things out, make logical deductions, stand back from his immediate feelings or envisage the abstraction of the future. He is firmly rooted in the present and what is actually happening to him. His reasoning has its own logic, both egocentric and magical. It's called pre-logical thinking. A child is a prisoner of the immediacy of his emotional response, without any distance or mediation via thought to put things into perspective or pinpoint the priorities and stakes involved. He is easily swamped by his feelings and needs our help to find his way out. On the other hand, he naturally looks for the meaning of whatever he is experiencing, doing it with the 'tool kit' he has on hand, according to his age and experience. He interprets and organizes his perceptions in his very own way, influenced by the often incomplete and sometimes deformed information he has at his disposal. And all this can give rise to emotions his parents are quite incapable of understanding as they reason from quite another 'data-base'.

Arnold is aggressive, and throws tantrums 'for nothing'. His parents have separated and he's living with his mother for the time being. Inside his mind he interpreted the situation, "Daddy has gone away = he doesn't love me because I'm a naughty boy."

Benedict is sad, isn't participating in class and doesn't play with the other children. She doesn't feel she belongs anywhere and always feels out of it. Her parents quarrel a lot. She said to herself, "Mommy and Daddy quarrel because of me. If I wasn't there, they wouldn't. It's all my fault."

Camilla fell ill with a serious and rapidly evolving leukemia. I came regularly to visit her at the hospital, once the connection established, to me he said what she had never said out loud but thought about so often, "My parents separated because of me. Before I was born, they were in love. It would be better if I were dead." Now, the illness has brought her parents together at her bedside.

Denis is afraid of people. His parents don't have friends in and go out very little, limiting themselves to home and family. Seeing that, he deduced: "The outside world is dangerous and people are not nice."

These conclusions are beliefs based on the feelings children have about themselves, their parents and life. They influence subsequent behavior. What children see, hear, feel can form a very confusing mental tangle. Such inextricable knots can cause more or less hurt, even to the extent of of blocking normal development in some way or other.

Children see the world through their own eyes and construe it accordingly. We mustn't pass judgement on their reactions. Let's just listen to them, try to identify what's going on and what associations are being made. Let's listen to what children say and what they feel.

So, he's afraid of a snail. What does a snail mean to him that he should be so afraid?

After having learnt a better way of listening, a client told me a story that happened with a little boy. Jason was sobbing his heart out because his balloon had burst in his hands. With what she had learnt, Elizabeth refrained from consoling him too quickly with the usual "Don't worry, I'll buy you another one." She came close to him and asked,"What's this balloon for you?" To her amazement, Jason looked up at her, and confided with a sob,"Everything dies. My grandpa died last week. "

And here are we grownups, thinking that the loss of a balloon is of no importance. If she had minimized the event, treating it as something very ordinary, without thinking any further, Elizabeth would have let a child's deep distress go by unnoticed. Since she was ready to listen, Jason was able to share his sadness.

Of course, all the children who cry because a balloon has burst in their hands have not just lost their grandpa. However, the metaphysical question has all-time validity. Parents tend to see the balloon and the small cost it represents. The child had a beautiful balloon in his hands, which suddenly disintegrated into a tiny bit of rubber sticking to his fingers. Such a transformation is brutal in itself. It also brings up the question of the power a child thinks he has or hasn't, and of the possibility of some form of guilt, especially if the parents react by saying, "You see, I told you to be careful!"

We have few means of assessing what is going on in a child's mind. So, let's be careful about minimizing what a child may feel. Some detail we haven't noticed may be of extreme importance in his eyes.

How can we listen and help untangle these emotional knots?

By letting children express their emotions and accompanying the discharge that tears, cries and trembling afford, without trying to calm them down. Crying and trembling are ways of expressing suffering, unwinding tension, 'letting off steam' and recovering from whatever form of emotional crisis is being played out. They know what is right for them. If you can just be there, listen and accompany the tears, calm will inevitably come after the storm, as well as a feeling of trust and physical well-being.

A baby will cry because he needs something or is trying to say something. First of all, ensure that all needs are satisfied. And then, if the crying continues, you can just tune into the tensions that are being shared. Maybe he's telling you that his birth was a fearful experience, that you weren't there at the right moment for the last feed… Maybe he doesn't feel accepted by his father… Maybe family mourning due to a relative's death is difficult to accept…There are so many possibilities for unhappiness, and in order to evacuate the resulting bodily discomfort he needs to cry it out. As the child grows and can put things into words. We must always listen to the emotions first and, above all, **take him seriously**. Better not ask *why* he's crying. We'll be given some sort of explanation which may be far from the actual difficulty. We can go along with what he's feeling by asking "What's going on?", "What's making you unhappy?" or even "What are you afraid of?"

His reasoning may seem illogical to an adult, but is in fact pre-logical, strongly felt and firmly believed in. We can help only by following the meanders of his thought process, contributing some missing information and looking at things from another angle.

Juliet is in kindergarten. She's the black sheep of the class. What's happened to make the other children so aggressive and scornful towards her? It's no use asking them to be 'nicer' to her. Behavior is a symptom and there are causes behind it. Let's look for them.

The teacher begins listening in and hears that Juliet is often insulted by the scornful: "You don't even have a daddy". These words are particularly violent for her as she lost her father hardly six months ago. The teacher remembered how Juliet had introduced herself on the first day of term by saying, straight off, "My name's Juliet and my daddy's dead." Matthew had instantly retorted, "It's not true! "For him, and for the other children, it was quite simply impossible that a father should die. That would imply that their own father could die and that was absolutely unthinkable. Why was this little girl saying something so awful? Who was this wicked girl suggesting something so ridiculous? She must be punished, hurt, destroyed.

The teacher got the children talking about it all, explored the way their minds were working and cleared up a few points, the reason for that particular father's death, his sickness and the idea that all this could be 'catching'. Those small children needed to know, for sure, that mixing with Juliet would not kill their own father. As if having a deceased father was something contagious. But that was the underlying idea which made the children panic, against which they fought by trying to exclude Juliet.

You may find yourself surprised and bewildered by the emotional intensity displayed by your child, or not understand what can cause such a reaction. You may be at a loss to know how to help him through the ordeal. You may just listen to what he's saying, putting yourself on his wavelength, seeing with his eyes, hearing with his ears with this question in mind,

**"What's he experiencing?"**

# 2

# What's being said?

Fred's teacher had just been imprisoned for the sexual abuse of children. A small boy had been assaulted over a period of four long months. His mother was surprised that he should have said nothing. However, when talking things over with the psychologist, she remembered him saying, "I've got tummy ache. I don't want to go to school." I thought he was just being difficult, trying to get out of going to school. And his teacher, Mr Whatsit, was so nice.

It's so often true that pedophiles are extremely 'nice'. Fred couldn't talk to his mother, she wouldn't listen. She misinterpreted his refusal, thought he was playing up and laid the blame on him, saying that he had such a nice teacher. By omitting to read meaning into her son's reluctance to go to school, she was pushing aside his needs.

Behind what parents will call 'playing up' and other strange, excessive, out-of-place or just un precedented behavior, let's seek out the emotions and the needs, because children are saying something in their own way.

If a child doesn't want to go to school, it's because there's some good reason. His teacher isn't necessarily a pedophile, but maybe his friend Sean isn't talking to him any more, or could he be afraid of his teacher or of that big boy in a higher class who comes to see him at break or of feeling stupid in his sports shorts in front of his classmates? He may not understand the lesson or may, quite simply, be bored by it. Whatever the case, he needs you, your understanding of what he is feeling, even your protection or your help to resolve some problem.

Behind all unusual behavior, particularly if it's systematic, lies a motivation, an emotional blockage and a hidden need. Excessive aggressiveness, submission, mother-dependency, jealousy, opposition and inability to concentrate are warning signs to be taken seriously.

Once again, it's better not to ask a child *why* he has done such and such a thing, because he usually doesn't know. It's more than likely that his deep-down motivation is completely unconscious. If you ask for a reason, he will very likely feel obliged to produce one and construct some plausible explanation. The one he offers is very rarely the real one.

A baby has no words to explain what is going on. His first language is crying. Little by little he'll learn to speak but what he can't say in words he will go on expressing by crying, shouting, stamping, using all sorts of 'loud' behavior to transmit his refusal to cooperate. It's not so easy to say what is going on inside ourselves, even for we adults. A child will probably not understand what is happening to him and also feel that it's forbidden to say anything anyway. He is afraid of his parents' reactions, their anger or sadness are equally difficult to assume.

Parents tend to label as 'capricious' the sort of difficult behavior they can't interpret. It's terrible for a child not to be understood and for his demands to be discredited. Capriciousness does not exist other than as a misunderstood form of language. The act of refusal offers a hidden code to be broken.

Of course it's not easy to capture the message coming from a child whose mind doesn't work like ours. But we've all had the experience of childhood and, with a little effort, we should be able to recall what we felt and how we tried to communicate.

Children close in on themselves when their various forms of refusal are not regarded as a search for communication, but met with disparaging comments like, "He always cries at this time of day", "he's always like that", "he's clumsy". In his as yet incomprehensible way, the child has been asking for something, seeking help or voicing a need, but hasn't been heard. So, he's forced into displaying a symptom, in order to make his point. Cases of recurrent otitis, eczema, allergies, refusal to eat, learning problems, aggressiveness… express underlying stress and can be interpreted as calls for help. The unconscious part of the child is ready to sacrifice growth, health and sanity in order to be heard.

However, not all children's behaviors are SOS messages. Don't be tempted to interpret all and everything, systematically seeking meaning in every word and gesture. All excess is harmful.

How can we know whether our child is saying something via an attitude, a sickness, an accident, a learning difficulty? Quite simply by listening to what he says.

You can be sure there's a message to be received when the behavior is repetitive, or if the physical symptoms last or reappear, despite treatment.

Don't be over-anxious about letting a message escape notice. As long as the problem hasn't been solved, it will repeat itself in a variety of ways or symptoms until a response has been provoked.

When a form of behavior surprises you, annoys you, worries you, or when an emotional response seems disproportionate or in systematic opposition, you may be sure there's a message. So, before the symptoms become alarming, your question will be,

**"What's being said?"**

# 3
# What's my message?

Be careful not to take anything and everything as a sub-liminal message! Writing on walls, scribbling on your diary, cutting up a curtain to make a wedding dress or princess outfit or drawing a football pitch on the new bedroom carpet are not necessarily behavioral warnings. They're just natural exploratory creative expressions. If things get damaged in the process, it's very likely not the primary intention, but rather the unforeseen consequence. It's all a question of age and awareness.

If your three-year-old daughter has just cut up one of your necklaces, it's obviously not the same thing as if your eight-year-old has done the same thing. The first one wonders what she can cut up with her new scissors, not having yet integrated the fact that it's irreversible and thinking that, anyway, it's doesn't matter because daddy can mend it. In the second case, it probably is a form of punishment, very likely expressing anger against you, your partner, her brother or sister, a teacher …

However, if a cut-up curtain really is transformed into a dress, don't destroy what could be an emergent talent! Maybe she's destined to become a famous dress-designer. I saw a Japanese multimillionnairess *haute couture* dress designer on TV. She set the fashion of everything pink – her favourite colour – from golf-balls to cars and everything around her. She started off in just that way – by cutting up curtains at home.

Ludovic very carefully drew a superb football field on his beautiful new green carpet. It was really well done. The carpet was his, it was in his room. He didn't know he wasn't supposed to do that, and after all it was his bedroom. His mother was able to acknowledge his talent, but his father shouted at him, obliging him to wipe it out immediately. In fact, his father would have been pleased to pay for an expensive carpet with a similar design but couldn't stand the fact that his son should do it himself and 'spoil' the carpet. He didn't for one minute look at the carpet objectively.

Our reactions towards our children's creations will condition their beliefs about themselves. What sort of message do you want to put out?

It could be either, "Oups! You're really creative and full of original ideas. But look, these colors stain the carpet. Wouldn't it be a good idea to find better raw materials to experiment with? Let's wipe out the colors with this sponge."

Or, "You're crazy! Don't you realize what you've done? You've made a complete mess!"

The child who receives the first message of encouragement will confidently use his competence in a creative way. The one who hears the second message, feeling humiliated and wrong, will continue to feel that way and seek revenge. It may be the carpet or some cherished collectible that gets damaged, or he may choose to destroy something in himself by self-depreciation, thinking he's stupid and of no value.

If you wish to teach him to respect things, respecting his vital need for expression is a necessity.

When I noticed felt-pen scribbles on the walls of my workroom, I was angry, and once more put up the notice for children, "Drawings must be done on paper, not on the walls." The graffiti continued, so I asked each child to do a drawing to decorate the walls of a corner of the room. Each child had thirty centimeters square for his personal expression, with the result that the corner of the room was most attractive – and the unwelcome scribbling ceased! This was our solution, as it was too difficult for me to persist in forbidding such decoration. My sister, a painter, had done wonderful frescoes on the staircase walls. Why should she be allowed to express herself and not the children? It wasn't fair! With their own space to decorate, they felt important and, happy with that, they didn't need to put their mark anywhere else.

Each time we react, we have the choice between a message of love, "I love you, you can do interesting things" or a message of detraction, "You're worthless, you can't do anything right."

## A common front?

A child has two parents. Logically, he has twice the chance of hearing positive messages. Alas! Sometimes, parents decide to 'find an agreement' and more often than not decide on a repressive attitude. Many parents think they should show their agreement and adhere to a common front. 'Front' is a term that conjures up a context of confrontation and stakes for power. No, children don't spend their time looking for the parental rift. They're looking for truth, happiness and fulfillment. They won't necessarily make the most of a difference of opinion between their parents. When one parent is heavy-handed and deals out a hurtful message, the other can supply an antidote. Children know what is fair and what isn't. It is far more inconsistent for a child to see one of his parents adopting the same attitude as the other on principle and thus betraying his personal values.

Imagine your partner has humiliated or hurt your child's feelings. You may say what you think, what you feel. Dare to take sides with the child, be a witness to his pain, defend him. He will know he can trust you. On the other hand, if you say nothing or uphold your partner's opinion, you are betraying your child and he'll trust you less. In the same way, accept that your partner should take his defence when you're the one to over-react. Nobody is perfect and we all make mistakes, speak before we think and 'let rip' because we're tired, exasperated or floundering in some traumatic throwback from our own childhood. Your image won't be tarnished in the eyes of your child, because he's looking for a real person rather than an image. By acknowledging your mistakes, you will teach him to admit his own.

Sometimes parents may not be in agreement, and it's important that the child should feel that. Why impose a one-track version of the world and of life? It's much more valuable to know that different opinions can co-exist. It leads to discussion, exchange and conflict-resolution.

So please, no common parental front! But neither any competition for who's right or wrong or the best parent nor raking other problems into the domain of upbringing!

Parents who talk about their differences of opinion with mutual respect are showing their offspring how to live together and love one another without always having to share the same ideas about everything.

## Our children observe us

Every word and deed carries a message for our children, whether addressed directly to them or to some other person or situation. Examining your life and the way you go about it means you can assess to what extent your life is an example of what you wish to transmit? Do you sometimes lie or perhaps hide or re-arrange reality for your own comfort? Do you respect rules and regulations, stop at traffic lights and pedestrian crossings? Is your behavior consistent with what you say should be done? And, in the more personal sphere, how much pleasure, love and happiness do you give out in everyday life? Are you stuck in a company, job, marriage or other partnership which doesn't suit you? What sort of message do you hand on when you talk about work, freedom, lifestyle, personal achievement and love?

To help you make choices concerning your attitudes with your children, you may ask yourself,

**"What's my message?"**

# 4

## Why am I saying that?

"Margot, Adrian, it's time to go!" I'm standing by the car and the children are picking up chestnuts from the side-walk, with their noses to the ground and pretending not to hear me.

"Hey! That one's for me!"

"Here another one for you! I put it in your pocket!"

I can feel myself getting impatient…and then I won-der,"Why on earth do I need them to get into the car right away? Is it just because it's what I've decided? What are my reasons? It's Sunday, I'm alone with them and have decided to spend the whole of this beautiful day all of us together. Okay, so it's lunchtime, but they don't seem particularly hungry. So why hurry? What's the difference between picking up chestnuts, going to the playground or having a go on the merry-go-round? Why not let them have fun on the sidewalk – for free!" We stayed another twenty minutes or so happily gathering up the gorgeous shiny brown chestnuts.

You've all come across this sort of situation of course. We react automatically and would do well to ask ourselves: "Why? What is making me say yes or no to my children's requests? Where does my attitude come from?"

The first time Margot wanted to eat her ice cream at the beginning of the meal, I heard myself say, "No, ice cream is a dessert and we eat it at the end of the meal. Wary of the automatic way I brought that out, I asked myself, "Why am I saying that?"

Looking at the situation rationally and scientifically, I remembered how digestion works and the way the stomach secretes insuline on receiving a dose of sugar, thus paving the way for digestion. If we eat sugar at the end of the meal, it's because we're greedy rather than hungry. So I let my daughter have her ice cream, and she ate up all her meal. Subsequently, she would eat fruit, a little ice cream or cake before pasta or green beans but less and less frequently as she grew up and more easily respected socially-accepted table manners. Occasionally she has wanted a bite of cake or a tangerine in the middle of the meal. Why should I forbid that since she eats up and over the week manages to get a balanced diet?

Moreover, science proves her right, except for the acidity of the tangerines which doesn't go well with the other food. Obviously, it's not good for children to be fed on ice cream. If there's too much they may not want their vegetables. Careful! Please don't think that I'm advising you to give your children their sweet course before the rest! But we always can think twice. What made me take that stance – health or habit? As a parent, I'm responsible for my child's health but also her social graces. However, we must be careful not to mix up the two messages by telling children that it's bad for them to eat dessert at the beginning of the meal.

What parents tend to fear if they give in to an unusual request from their child, is that it will become a whim. This is an adult invention and crops up when parents trip themselves up in their own power games. When Margot asked for ice cream at the beginning of the meal, she was not being capricious but exploratory. If I had asserted my authority and refused the idea, she would probably have dug her toes in. I do believe that power games are started by the parents, not the children, since they are totally dependant on us and don't have the mental capacity.

Does our behavior result from our education, automatic reactions whose origin we ignore, what seems obvious or rational thinking? By the latter, I mean honest reasoning derived from reliable information, not the heavily biased opinions doled out by our parents or family doctor.

We must be wary of the deformed information that we are served up via advertizing.

One mother told me how hard she had had to fight so that her son would eat up his daily yoghurt. Victim to advertizing, she thought it was not just good, but necessary for him to eat dairy products. The food industry messages were so strong that she was unable to listen to her son. When she discovered less-orientated information, she was able to acknowledge her mistake. She had been forcing her son to eat the acidifying yoghurt instead of letting him eat the almonds and hazel nuts that he loved and which would give him far more calcium. In fact, what she had thought was necessary was not really that good!

The last time we went on holiday, I was flabbergasted to see a short but edifying scene in the hotel. We were lining up at the buffet and everybody could choose one of two dishes. That day, Francforter sausages or *cordon bleu* chicken were on the menu. A little girl alongside her father insisted that she wanted the sausages, but her father refused, saying, "Mom said *cordon bleu* and *cordon bleu* it will be." It's true that sausages are not exactly a health food, but the *cordon bleu* is just fried chicken (battery-reared), topped with a slice of ham and a bit of cheese. It can be very tasty, admittedly, but three proteins all together and high fat are not a good idea diet-wise. What the little girl wanted was no worse, so why not let her have it? Such absurdity and lack of awareness leave one speechless. The little girl accepted her lot, in spite of her ten years or so. Her mother obviously ruled over her life without wondering about the validity of her decisions. It's impossible to be all-knowing, but when our children ask for things we're about to refuse why not listen and, before answering, wonder

**"Why am I saying that?"**

# 5

# Do my needs compete with those of my children?

We would like our children to stop crying for 'nothing', not to throw a tantrum because we refuse them something or even because we have the impertinence to think of changing their dirty nappy.

We would like our children to be more co-operative, get dressed when we ask them to, come and have whatever meal is on the table at the same time as everyone else, go to bed without arguing, tidy up their bedroom, hang up their clothes in the right place and put away their shoes in the closet.

We would like them not to shout and run about all over the place, but be quiet and well-behaved, sit down on their chair at the table, eat up their meal properly with a knife and fork and without dragging out the process, drink without spilling the water or trying out physics experiments concerning fluid mechanics...

In fact, we would like our children to stop acting like children!

However, the fact is that they are children and, as such, they are behaving like children when they throw their toys all over the place, walk barefoot on the tile floor, get up at dawn to play, shout at the top of their lungs, hide in cupboards and run around the living room, or even mess up the kitchen with their muddy boots.

To be perfectly honest, wouldn't we be rather uneasy if they really did behave like miniature adults – neat and obedient? After a few minutes of admiration tinged with envy, we would soon be disturbed by their lack of spontaneity.

We must admit though, that children's and parents' needs are diametrically opposed. Most parents like a degree of order, peace and quiet, well-reasoned dialogue, and mornings in bed. Most children are happy with in a state of disorder, love noise and get up at dawn, especially on Sunday mornings though during the week that seems to be more difficult!

The situation is necessarily oppositional and cannot but complicate the relationship. As soon as we take stock of the disparity of needs, rival demands are likely to collide head-on. In power games there is a winner but also a loser. If we look at this in terms of the relationship, there are inevitably two losers. How can you feel appreciated by someone who denies your needs?

Being a parent implies putting aside your personal needs to satisfy those of such vulnerable little beings. But it's neither simple nor easy. One desperate young mother confided to me that she was sometimes so beyond herself that she felt like hitting her child and, totally taken aback, was horrified by the thought. Before becoming a mother, she had imagined children as perfectly angelic little things that she would never cease to admire. Later, she was astonished to find herself exasperated by their behavior and her ability to detest them.

Of course they drive us mad, make us lose control. All parents have one hell of a time... unless they give their children a hell of a time!

According to their age, nights are sliced up by feedings, bed-wetting or nightmares. In the daytime, the little ones demand constant attention and the bigger ones squabble. It's impossible to delve into a book, quietly chat with a friend on the phone, laze in bed in the morning or even go to the toilet in peace and quiet. Living with children is really testing and if we don't face that, we'll stock up whole lot of grudges and hard feelings which will spill over at the slightest upset, "Tristan, you're a pest!" or even, "What ever have I done to deserve such a child?"

Parenting is a full-time, round-the-clock occupation. If some take eight or ten hours off to go and work, they have to pick up the task when they get back home. It's quite restful in the office, with status and adult companionship – no crying, shouting or fighting – quite a relief really. Mothers who don't work outside the home don't have that breathing space to get away for a while and do something different. Indeed, work can be very fulfilling unless it's not according to one's choice. At work, it's possible to feel competent and appreciated, at least by one's colleagues and it's a place to gain confidence. Even when the job isn't fabulous it affords an opportunity for contact and exchange with others.

If we don't acknowledge our needs but feel deprived of something that would nourish our own development, we will very probably find it difficult to nourish our children's needs. **It really is a parental duty to identify our own needs and satisfy them as far as possible**.

When there is a conflict of interests, competition isn't the only option. **Co-operation pays and is always the best long-term choice.** Once again, sincere expression of one's needs is a pre-requisite, along with mutual respect. We must to recognize other people's needs *and* assert our own.

Once the infant-stage (when children's needs are paramount) is over, learn to negotiate. **Those much-discussed limits are the ones imposed by your needs.**

"I really need some peace and quiet for my meal. How can you help me?" is so much more effective than, "Be quiet, you're such a nuisance!" or worse...

If they don't want to go to bed, you can tell them that it's parents' time and that you're not going to bother with them. Its a waste of time threatening, telling off or punishing – it's more efficient to just protect your needs because in that way your child will be willing to help you.

It's so important to get enough rest so as to avoid getting rundown and enough enjoyment so as to be available. Task-sharing done on an equal basis prevents parents from bearing unconscious grudges. **Acknowledging one's anger and frustration – that feeling of unfairness** when the other partner is not there to take their share (whether for some external reason, separation or just non-cooperation) helps avoid taking it out on the children. If parents don't recognize their emotions and needs, they risk projecting inappropriate attitudes on the children.

Patricia has brought up two children alone. Worried by the lack of a father she tried to compensate by giving them a double-dose of attention. Another reality hit her when she started thinking things over – a man was lacking in her life. She had refused to admit that for a long time, projecting that lack on her children. At the present time, she is finding it difficult to make them independent. They lack confidence and remain very dependant on their mother.

No mother, however attentive and loving, can ever replace a father. It's not her role. Children don't expect her to remove the difficulty and provide what's missing, but do expect her to listen to their feelings and not deny her own. If she had paid attention to her own needs, Patricia would have let her children grow up with more freedom and maybe met a man to play the role of a father. A masculine element would have contributed the stabilizing presence her sons needed.

**To listen to one's own needs is not selfish behavior. It's taking stock of the situation, facing reality, and acting accordingly. Usually it brings satisfaction to all parties.**

## When our parents are obstacles between us and our children

Although our daily life brings its inevitable load of worries and problems, our most exacting and urgent needs date back from a long time ago. **Our most uncontrollable needs are those stemming from our childhood experiences.** Since they usually went, not only unsatisfied but unnoticed as such, the lacks are perpetrated. Our emotions easily take over, competing with and making us deaf to our own children's needs, and then we become unable to understand or react appropriately.

"She makes me mad with all her whining!" Maryse is incapable of being tender with her daughter because her own parents never took her in their arms. In spite of her conscious wish, the barrier is too great and she just can't manage to do it. When Eve comes up close and asks for a cuddle, she is pushed away. To accept would be to see Eve being cuddled and thus imagine herself receiving what she did not receive – impossible! She was so unhappy at not being cuddled that she can't bear to awaken the painful souvenir of that lack. She prefers to deny her own need ("I wasn't cuddled and it didn't kill me") and also that of her daughter in order to bury the whole issue. For if she admitted that her daughter needed a cuddle, she would logically have think that all little girls do too, and that she as a child would have had that need.

**When childhood emotions are repressed, we are unable to perceive the real needs of our children. Either we unconsciously project our own needs, magnified by years of frustration or deny their needs to avoid our personal suffering.**

So Maryse came to ask herself, "Do I really want to put myself before my daughter?" Of course not!

A fortnight after giving birth, Nathalie went skiing and gave her baby to her grandmother to look after. She justified her behavior by saying that she needed to rest and get back to normal after the ordeal. She had no idea of what her baby could feel. After talking it through, it was discovered that she had been separated from her mother very young. She had buried the pain, the anger and the terror, ending up by inflicting the same ordeal on her daughter, as if to say to her mother, "You were quite right, you see, I came through it all right and I'm doing the same as you to *my* daughter."

Kathryn went abroad for two months for her job, leaving her three-month old son in France with a nanny, certified of course, but whom she had never met before. On her return, she didn't understand why Tom was literally wasting away. He had refused to eat and slept badly. He had stopped his development. Despite appearances, Kathryn hadn't keyed into her own needs by going away like that. She had, in fact, listened to the sirens of her own childhood, for she had been abandoned by her mother at that very same age.

Clara is the mother of three children and Diego the father of two, but they both tend to get home late from work. They admit that behind the workload there is also the reluctance to face the children, with their demands and emotions. Work is definitely easier. The children make out as best they can with television and video games. Each of their parents is fleeing the contact with his own childhood.

Babies can't satisfy their needs by themselves. When the adults on which they depend are not available because they're revisiting the emotional prisons of their own childhood, they find themselves in great distress. Babies and small children readily accept to comply and adapt, so as to be in the good graces of whoever is parenting in order to survive, be accepted and loved. They learn how not to cry if nobody comes to get them; they learn how to suck more slowly if they notice the force of the sucking is a worry for their mother. They repress needs and expressions of affection, become very *good* and the pride of their parents. But, in order to do this, they shelve their emotions, learn that they can't trust people and that the outside world is, first and foremost, a hostile place.

On the other hand, if the parents attend to their true needs (both within their couple and as an individual) and if the former wounds are healed, they will be able to attend to the needs of their children.

No book or expert can ever give universal answers. Each child is a different person, unlike anyone else on Earth. What is more, children change and evolve, whether this concerns their shoe size or other needs. A child can love going into the water at the age of two but be very fearful when three at the simple idea of putting a toe into the sea.

There's no infallible recipe, no systematic strategy, no guarantee. It's always a question of adaptation and it can be difficult when one's own childhood has been forgotten.

To live happily together, let's try to contain our children's excesses within the limits we find tolerable, and then try to extend those limits. We mustn't forget that they depend on us, that we are the providers. Let's try to heal our old wounds so as to allow a free rein to our children's energies and rhythms. We'll all gain in ease and pleasure.

When we're exasperated by our children, incapable of responding or tempted to overprotect, and also if they're too good, or on the contrary too boisterous, we can ask ourselves,

**" Are my needs competing with those of my children? "**

# 6

# What's most important for me?

Beatrice, who's two, is sobbing her heart out. Her glass slipped from her hands and her mother shouted at her – but she didn't do it on purpose!

Hubert, seven, shuts himself up in his room, making as little noise as possible. He's scared stiff that his father will find all the papers on his desk stuck together. It's not his fault – he just tried to stick a broken toy back together again, one he stepped on by accident. Knowing that if he told his father, he would lecture him saying something like, "If you'd put your things away, this wouldn't have happened", he preferred trying to repair the damage. That's when it all went wrong. He was busy holding all the bits together when the cat jumped up and knocked the pot of glue all over the papers.

Parents too often fly off the handle with their children, telling them off and completely forgetting who or what is most important. When a broken vase, a spilled glass of milk, a piece of clothing dropped on the living-room floor sets off an orgy of shouting, taking the risk of making our child feel insecure, it's as if we were more concerned by the vase, the flower bed, the sofa than by our children. That's the message they are likely to get.

"What is most important for me?" is the first question to ask oneself before saying or doing anything, in order to get things into proportion. Parents are adults and possess a brain able to defer automatic emotional reactions and can choose the appropriate behavior according to their values and aims. A child's brain is not yet able to do that.

If I reply, "My children's love and trust are the most important things to me and I don't want to ever be ashamed of my behavior in front of them", then I will be protecting that love and that trust.

It's not the same if I reply that my mother-in-law's opinion, cleanliness in my kitchen or my personal comfort are the most important for me, in which case I will be protecting my image of a good mother, daughter-in-law or housewife or just my peace and quiet.

This choice is rarely conscious, and thus all the stronger. Your child is tuned into your unconscious mind and your reactions are more powerful than words. If you are exasperated by a broken glass or a stain on his shirt, you're humiliating and wounding him and, logically, he'll think that the glass or the shirt are more important than he is. In spite of the words "I love you darling" murmured at other moments, he may integrate the message, "I'm not important for Mommy", or "I'm only loved if I'm perfect, if I'm not myself".

Becoming aware of what prompts our reactions towards our children can radically modify our behavior.

Theodora has a terrible relationship with her mother, who humiliated and belittled her throughout her childhood. She now has her own children and her mother behaves in the same abusive way with her grandchildren. She neglects the elder boy and noisily shows her preference for his younger brother, giving him presents and taking him to the zoo or the cinema. Theodora was scared stiff of her mother and for a long time said nothing. By asking herself the question of what was most important, she realized that she was protecting her mother – or to put it more exactly, hoping that she would end up by being loved by her, inevitably to the detriment of her children. That was enough to make her realize that her children's happiness was more precious than her submission to her mother, who rapidly stopped her destructive behavior when she saw her daughter's determination.

Children inevitably upset their parents' way of doing things. It's the way of the world. If the latter don't accept that but continue living the same way as before, as if they didn't have children and could go on with the same life and work modes as before, the children will conclude that they are of no importance. If they feel intrusive, with no right to be there, they are likely to develop a feeling of shame ("I'm a nuisance") and inferiority ("I'm not good enough").

Children need to feel that they're precious, that they are welcome and that their needs are taken into account.

"What's most important for me?" This question helped me on numerous occasions. For example, when the peony I had planted in the middle of the garden was assaulted by little runaway legs, when the work I had just done on my computer was lost by inquisitive two-year-old fingers playing with the keyboard... or simply when I was tired and found myself having to bend down to wipe the floor.

There is not a shadow of doubt that the most important things for me are the love and trust for and from my children. It's important not to humiliate, hurt or terrorize them. In all circumstances I want to be honest, open about my feelings and able to understand what they feel. It's the way to help them love one another, feel proud of their talents and assume their responsibilities without feeling guilty.

When our children disturb our lives and we don't know how to react, when we know that we are not acting for their benefit but as our parents did or as people expect us to, we should ask ourselves,

**"What's most important for me?"**

# 7

# What's my aim?

There's no absolutely good or bad way of doing things, just the one that gets me where I want to be and the one that doesn't. I don't take the same road to go to Spain or Germany. And then there are highways and byways which are more or less direct and take more or less time to get wherever we've decided to go.

Is it good or bad to let your child choose the clothes he wants to wear today?

Is it good or bad to consent to a child's demand?

Is it good or bad to let children cry?

Is it good or bad to put them to bed at 8 o'clock?

In fact, nothing is good or bad, it's just a question or getting closer to what you're aiming at. One day you'll say *yes*, another you'll say *no*, according to your child's evolution and needs, and according to your objective. With children, rather than giving or taking outside advice on what is 'good' or 'bad', it's primordial for the parents to know where they're going, "What's my aim here and now in my relationship with my child?"

Karen has just received a pair of roller skates for her birthday. Geraldine, her older sister, who's eight, wants some too. Their mother, Susan, says 'no', but that she would give her some for her birthday two months ahead. However, Summer holidays are on the horizon and it would be nice for both girls to be able to skate together. But then Karen would find the situation unfair to her. Susan wonders what to do, weighs up the pros and cons and come to me for advice. I suggest she should ask herself, "What's my aim?' Her relationship with her elder daughter is difficult, as Geraldine is very jealous of her sister – and not without reason, admits her mother. It has always been easier dealing with Karen. That's normal, she's her second child. Susan talks to me about Geraldine's birth and their particulat mother-daughter story. She feels unhappy about not having been able to show as much love to the first as to the second daughter. Should she tell Geraldine how much she loves her, how important she is for her? What *should* she do? I say nothing. Susan went out and bought skates for Geraldine that very evening, telling her that they were a way of showing her love to repair the past. Susan had listened to her heart and Geraldine had understood. It was an important moment for both of them.

Another situation or another aim will inevitably cause another reaction. There is no universal answer, just one for whichever child and whichever parent are in dialogue at that precise moment of their life together. All our acts are dictated by more or less conscious objectives. It may so happen that we have behavior that goes against our conscious aims. Like Pamela. She says she wants her children to grow up and be able to think for themselves, but every evening she lays out the clothes she wants them to wear the next day. Our aims determine our behavior and thus our relationship with our children, and all the more so if they remain unconscious. So, becoming aware of them enables us to better choose how we act and create the sort of relationships we want.

If I want an impeccable kitchen, I won't behave as I would if my aim were to teach my children that they can trust me in all circumstances.

If my objective is to reassure my child about my love for him, I won't behave in the same way if my aim is to help him grow up and face frustration.

If my objective is to prove to my husband that I'm a perfect and irreproachable wife, I won't behave in the same way if I want to be attentive to the needs of my children.

As long as I'm bothered about somone else's judgement, whether real or imaginary, I won't be centred on my children's real needs.

Considering children's needs to be important and putting them first doesn't mean letting them do anything or saying nothing when they do damage. It means showing my feelings but letting them know that my love is absolute.

I particularly loved a very beautiful, hand-made glass, decorated with a blue snake, that my partner had given me. The children were forbidden to touch it. A moment's inattention was enough for Adrian (two) to seize the glass and let it slide from his fingers. When the vase shattered on the tiles of the kitchen floor, I burst into tears. I loved that glass, but I remained conscious of my love for my children and of my aim – to transmit that my love was unconditionnel and that they could trust me. So, I was able to express my anger without blaming my son who, as I saw through my tears, was already shocked by the shattered glass. Seeing my reaction, Adrian started to cry. I was able to reassure him, tell him that I still loved him but that I needed to cry because I was upset at the breakage. **I talked about me not about him**. I showed my feelings without judging him. Subsequently, he said several times, "Once, I broke your glass, and you cried and I cried too. It was as if he needed to recall the incident in order to digest it." Each time, I would answer, "Yes, I cried because I loved the glass and couldn't drink out of it any more, and it's normal to cry when you've lost something you loved." A few months later, Adrian put a big glass down on the table very carefully, "You see Mommy, I didn't break it, because last time I broke your glass and you cried. I don't like it when you cry. I cried too because I had broken your glass. You cried and I cried too." Adrian is now much more careful when handling things. He says it himself, and has become aware of what the loss of a cherished object can mean to me or to others. He had felt guilty, but with a healthy feeling of guilt which pays attention to other people's feelings and the consequences of acts and which guided towards greater responsibility.

If I had told him off, told him he was clumsy or shouted at him, he would most likely have felt not just unhappy, but bad. He would have felt a harmful feeling of guilt and shame, turning the anger he naturally felt against himself as a protection from the humiliation, but impossible to voice because he was the one at fault. Having accepted and integrated the fact that he was clumsy or careless, he would in the future pay more attention to *being careful* than to *taking care* of things. Feeling tense, he would concentrate on his possible clumsiness and failure and inevitably cause some mishap. And then, after another mishap, he would be confirmed in the idea that he really was clumsy and careless.

When you're convinced you're clumsy, you're far more likely to damage something than when you're sure of being adroit. Are you wanting to teach your child to be careless or careful? In fact, if you treat your children as if they were the most precious things for you, your fragile possessions will be much safer. A child who knows he's precious will be attentive to other people and to the consequences of his acts. He won't be moved by fear of 'doing things wrong' but with respect for other people's feelings and responsibility for other people's things. So,

**"What's my aim?"**

# 8
# Seven questions to remember

*What's he experiencing?*

*What's being said?*

*What's my message?*

*Why am I saying that?*

*Do my needs compete with those of my children?*

*What's most important for me?*

*What's my aim?*

# Chapter III

## Life is movement

It's not always easy to listen to children's emotions. They disturb us, threaten the image we have of ourselves as a good mother or father. They are destabilizing and we wonder, "What should I do?" Instead of having a protective rôle, we find ourselves mere providers. To be frank, we would all prefer that our children did not cry, shout or roll on the floor. We would rather they didn't feel and express so many emotions.

However, their emotions are their most precious asset, as that's where their sense of identity comes from, where the inner feeling of their own existence takes root.

A child who is 'as good as gold' certainly stays still, but has also let something die deep down. Life is movement. A picture stays still, so to resemble it a child must repress the movement within himself. E-motion – E = towards the exterior, motion = movement. Emotion means the movement of life from the inside to the outside of oneself.

Fear serves the cause of anticipation and survival. Sadness marks loss and mourning. Joy is an expansive feeling and spurs us on. Anger defines our limits, our rights, our personal space and our integrity, and results from frustration. Love links us to others.

Crying, shouting, stamping and trembling are tension-relievers. A child's life is full of doubts, fears, frustration and anger…all babies need to cry, however well-cared for they may be. Emotions help us recover and give us the opportunity of healing after something that has hurt. All painful events, accidents, ordeals or injustice are not traumatic unless we're not allowed to freely express the feelings they cause. Free-flowing emotions guarantee our mental health. Emotions are not popular, but they are fundamental. They endow awareness of our existence.

# 1

# Who am I? Someone with emotions

The key to awareness is our capacity for emotions.

"Hello young man!"

"I'm not a young man, I'm Adrian."

Adrian, just two years and two months old (precocious, we must admit) does not approve of being defined. He's been insisting on saying his name for the last few days. When I come to put food in his plate and say:

"May I serve you sir?"

He replies, "I'm not a sir, I'm Adrian."

Adrian exists. He asserts his identity, his individuality and the life force in him by expressing what he wants and doesn't want, what he feels, what he's experiencing.

"**I'm** very angry, very angry, because I'm angry."

"**I'm** sad when you go away. I don't want you to go away."

"Oh Mommy, **I'm** so glad to see you!"

"When **I** poured the salt cellar into my mouth, it burnt. **I** cried."

When a child announces, "**I** don't want to go to sleep", we're tempted to say: "Well, that's the way it is. It's bedtime, no two ways about it".

Or maybe to reason, "You need to sleep to feel fit tomorrow morning."

Or maybe to explain, "You know, I have to go to work."

We reply and try to settle the problem, but don't listen to what the child is saying. In fact, in all these cases he's not asking for anything. He's exploring the **I** sentences and fashioning the idea of being a subject – a 'first person'. He's just saying who he is – ME!

He's expressing feelings, formulating what is going on inside him, telling us who he is and what he's experiencing. He is experimenting with the pure feeling of his existence, so why should we talk about anything else? If we respond to the content rather than tuning into the emotion or feeling, we're letting the child know that he's not important, that his ME is negligible. Behind our rational explanations, he will understand that he *shouldn't* be feeling what he *is* feeling!

How is it that we react in such an insensitive way? Have we pushed our own emotions so far away that we would rather not contact them? Would we rather remain unmoved? Are we afraid that our repressed feelings surge up and invade our lives?

What happened to us at the same age? Scared of bringing a painful past to the surface, we manage to refuse understanding of our children's assertions and protestations. In this way, we are shutting them in behind the same bars as ourselves.

Why don't we make the most of the opportunity to follow them where they are taking us, step out of our prison and leave them their freedom to **BE**?

To listen to and validate a children's feelings is to help them build up their character and exist as individuals.

Who am I? I am **ME.**

The feeling of being onself depends on emotional awareness. I am the person I *feel* myself to be.

If a child doesn't have the right to express what she feels, if no one listens to her tears, her fears or her fury and if no one confirms that what she feels is founded and that she has the right to feel that, then she may go to the extent of removing from her conscious mind what she really *is* feeling. Either she ceases to feel anything, or she takes on another feeling – one that is allowed – instead of her inner truth.

When children have no right to experience their own feelings, they remain defined by their parents, their teachers... others. These become the ones who tell them who they are and they obediently take on the designated role. They're no longer in contact with their own sense of Beingness.

# 2

## "So anything goes?"

This little phrase is used to defeat the argument.

It reflects a complete absence of understanding concerning children's emotions and needs. **No, listening to and respecting children's emotions does not imply systematically satisfying their demands.**

There we are at the circus. All sorts of winking, blinking hats and fluorescent gadgets are being sold as we go in. Margot pulls on my arm and says, "Mommy, I want one of those."

"No, I don't want to buy you one, it costs too much!" I unthinkingly reply.

"I know you won't buy it for me, but I still have the right to want one!"

Most certainly, she had the right to want one. I had let myself pronounce a ritual reply.

The question of frustration is everpresent as we go through life with children.

Between permissive parents who frustrate as little as possible and the authoritative ones who have no complexes about it, where do children's needs lie?

# Resisting temptation

In his book *Emotional Intelligence* (1995, *Bantam Books*) Daniel Goleman cites an experiment on four-year-olds led by a psychologist, Walter Mischel. The children were given the following choice: "In the room, there is a box with a marshmallow in it. If you take it, you'll just have the one. If you wait till I come back I'll give you two."

About a third of the children jumped on the marshmallow a soon as he went out. Two thirds of them waited till he came back and got two. Since this experiment was carried out in a Stanford University daycare group, it was possible to follow the children during their schooling.

Twelve or so years later, the differences on a psychological level between the impulsive ones and the others were spectacular. Those who had resisted temptation were more confident, efficient and able to cope with difficulty. They were less vulnerable when in doubt and when facing fear or failure, coped better with stress and knew how to achieve their aims in spite of obstacles.

The children who helped themselves to the marshmallow right away had a more disturbed profile. More stubborn, but less decisive, they avoided contact with others, were easily upset when things didn't go as planned and tended to abandon tasks when difficulties arose. At the end of their secondary school studies, the first group showed themselves to be the better-performing pupils. Their results were twenty percent better than those of their classmates. Knowing how to resist an impulse and delay satisfaction are abilities that serve ulterior development. A child's performance at four is predictive of future capacities. Drug addicts and delinquents are noted for being people who cannot stand frustration. The least obstacle to their desires is felt to be a serious affront.

So the interpretation of these results was obvious: frustration-tolerance could determine your future. But was it really the case? After decades of this belief being upheld, it was challenged by a woman researcher. She discovered that the children who ate the marshmallow right away were in fact very clever and adaptative. They came from families they couldn't trust. Their parents' promises were not always held. Their needs were not always met. So their attitude had finally nothing to do with frustration-tolerance, but more with knowing they couldn't trust adult promises. They had learned a hard lesson: "Better take what I can have now, the future is too uncertain." They were indeed reacting according to their experience of adult behavior. Consequently, drug addicts and delinquents are not necessarily people who haven't learned to cope with frustration but people whose childhood needs were not met, who were lied to, who learned that others were not to be trusted, who frequently felt powerless and lacked grounding.

Nonetheless, the aptitude to manage frustration, defer satisfaction and subordinate the present to the future are the fundamentals of being able to find happiness. They are the valuable tools in life that enable us to carry out our projects and favour good relationships with others.


## How does a child learn how to deal with her feelings of frustration?

Making a child feel frustration on purpose can only fail to help her become a person. Letting a baby cry, refusing to pick her up or cuddle an older child or taking away a present were often former parental strategies so as not to spoil us but to harden us. Such methods have consequences. Children develop a particular sensitivity to frustration, and any delaying of immediate satisfaction becomes intolerable, leading to intense worry which they will try to control by becoming dependent on some outside element: alcohol, drugs, a partner or some other form of compulsive behavior which makes them become blind to their real needs.

Some people, when they saw me breastfeeding my children on demand, responding to their needs, refusing to let them cry alone in their bedroom, warned us that we were on the road to making them into wimps, unable to cope with their frustration. In fact I can see that, young as they were, they both managed their frustration remarkably, even surprisingly well.

In Sweden, an interesting study showed a remarkable reduction of tooth decay by limiting children to just one candy day per week. I found the idea interesting, not only for preserving their teeth, but also for putting non-repressive limits on sugar consumption. So I suggested the idea to my two and four year olds.

We chose Saturday as candy day and the whole family was informed, so that no well-intentioned grandmother or uncle would offer too much temptation. If however, they did receive candy on other days, then they were invited to keep it for Saturdays. If they chose to eat their candy, then that was their business – they knew I wouldn't be pleased, and that was usually enough to limit rule-breaking. I just expressed my disapproval but didn't punish them or tell them off. They knew that they didn't have to 'obey' me, that it was an open contract between us.

Usually, Margot, when she got candy, would give it to me till the following Saturday. On occasion, I would see her hurriedly pop something in her mouth or rush into her room to hide something. One or two small exceptions were nothing compared to the importance of what was being learnt. She had to feel free to eat or wait – it was her choice. Otherwise, facing the frustration would not have been her own decision!

Even Adrian, at two and a half, carefully hid away three sweeties he had received from his baby-sitter until the following Saturday. Once, he managed to keep a lollipop offered in a restaurant and give it to me like his sister, after a drive all the way home. Nonetheless, on Saturday his first words were, "I want my lollipop."

## Needs and wants

Since the well-known, pioneering French child psychologist, Françoise Dolto, we know how too much frustration can be traumatic, but also that it is inevitable and helps us grow up. There are desires and needs and the two are not equivalent. Children don't *need* that red car or blond dolly but, understandably, they *want* them. On the other hand, they have a true *need* that their anger (expression of their frustration) be heard and respected. Obviously, we mustn't say yes to anything and everything. It's formative to face a (justified) refusal.

Is your child rolling on the ground in fury? She doesn't *need* the candy even though she *wants* it terribly. She needs to express her frustration and wants her fury to be understood. It's important, because she needs to check that your refusal doesn't separate you from her. You said no and she can easily fear that the relationship is in danger and be over-whelmed by the intensity of her feelings. She's screaming, but look at her – she's trying to hit you, seeking contact. If you avoid that, she'll hit a wall or some object, trying to re-establish the relationship. It's important not to deprive her of the contact at the very moment she needs it most.

During the intermission of a show we'd gone to see, Margot looked at the balloons being sold in the aisles, "Mommy, I want a balloon!" I could have said no, explaining to her by saying, "I can't always be buying things. Those balloons cost too much." Or lie, "I don't have enough money left." Or distract her, "Let's have a look at the programme and you can show me how well you can read." Remembering her remark earlier on, I looked at the balloons. I found them beautiful too. I exclaimed, "I like the one with the parrot best. Oh look! There's Simba the lion cub with his daddy." She followed on, "I like the pink mermaid best!" We talked about what we liked, and a little boy nearby joined in the game, "There's Mickey too…" We had a nice time talking and fantasizing. No more need to buy the ballon, the desire for a balloon had disappeared with the satisfaction of the need for contact, for sharing.

Please don't imagine anything systematic here. Satisfying wants for candy and presents is not toxic in itself. To refuse all such things, just because they're not *needs*, would be unfair. Children would end up thinking that pleasure is forbidden, with all the consequences it could have on the rest of their lives. It's worth remembering that candy and balloons, whether given or refused, are not to be taken at face value but as pretexts for learning how to relate. Do we really want to let a piece of candy spoil our relationship with our children?

Frustration is inevitable in life, so it's not worth adding on more than necessary. Some day or another, you will frustrate your child, whether for her protection or her health or just in order to respect your own needs.

The heart of the matter is to go along with her way of experiencing frustration and to accept listening to her anger.

# 3

# "I just don't understand him"

## A mixed message

Margot is squabbling with her brother. They're playing at Indians with little figurines and she wants the little grey horse that her brother is jealously holding on to, not the brown one he's handing over. It's a dead-end situation. She's crying, insisting on having the horse she cannot have. So, what's going on behind the scenes?

I widen my view of the situation: Margot's godmother is sitting on the sofa and talking with her daddy. Now, a few minutes ago, when we went upstairs to put on her pyjamas, Margot confided to me, "I want a cuddle with my godmother because I don't see her a lot." When we came down the latter was busy talking and Margot, not wanting to interrupt, started playing quietly nearby, waiting for an invitation. The hoped-for signal didn't come and she felt left out and frustrated. It was impossible to express the real reason for that without taking the risk of being rejected. So, she expressed her frustration by turning on her brother for the horse she was not being given. She gave her brother the very message she wanted to express to her god-mother.

The meaning was clear, "You don't give me what I want."

## Getting the message over by inversing roles

After the Christmas holidays, Lucile is crying, "I don't want to go back to school, I don't have any friends."

Her mother doesn't understand, "What are you talking about? You've got lots of friends, Alexandra, Chloe, Nuria, Saïda and Camilla are all your friends aren't they?"

"They don't want to play with me any more."

"That's not true. Chloe invited you to come over last Wednesday, you're going to Camilla's next week and whenever I come to school, I find you playing with one or other of them."

Lucile swallows her tears and, resignedly returns to school. Once again, let's move back to take a better look at the situation. Lucile says she doesn't have any friends although she has plenty. So, maybe she isn't talking about herself, but saying *I* because her mother doesn't hear her when she says *you*. And there, Lucile is right. Her mother Marianne, doesn't make deep friendships. Although she's sociable and vivacious on the surface, Marianne doesn't really like herself very much. As soon as the first contact has been established, she moves away in case people discover who she really is, or thinks she is: somebody who's a bit boring and doesn't have anything to say.

Marianne and Lucile went away together during the holidays. They laughed together and shared things. The little girl saw her mother happy, far from the sadness she expressed rather too often. Lucile didn't want her mother to be alone again because it was the beginning of term. She was, in fact, trying to tell her mother that it would be a good thing to make friends, but her mother had laughed it off by saying, "I've had friends, but at the moment I don't have. That's the way it goes." Not so happy about going to school without saying any more, Lucile tried to get over one last message by transposing the problem onto her own life. Her mother didn't understand because it was obvious that her daughter had friends, and she didn't realize that she was trying to tell her to get down to making friends too!

Once again, capricious behavior doesn't exist. If you don't understand what your child is saying, then dig down deeper. Try to find out what's going on. What need is she expressing? Is she trying to say something about someone other than herself? Listening to the message and then opening your eyes to examine the whole scene and what's going on in the wings will help you figure out what or who is being addressed?

## My baby cries for no reason

Crying is associated with suffering. In fact, as researcher Dr. Aletha Solter[2] explains that crying is a natural therapy. It's an effort that the body contributes to its reconstruction and is fundamentally therapeutic! Crying lowers blood pressure, eliminates toxins, relaxes muscular tension and re-establishes proper breathing. After a really good bout of sobbing, we feel relaxed and liberated.

Psychotherapy partly consists of expressing repressed emotions from the past in order to come closer to our true being. After recalling a painful memory, I invite people to 'cry it out'. Babies, like us all, need to cry it out. Crying is not always motivated by immediate needs, but may be the expression of accumulated tension and complaints about past suffering. For example, when birth has been difficult, the baby may need to moan about the pain or fear she felt at the time, sometimes weeks later.

Babies have a great need for tenderness, contact, carrying, smells and cuddling. A baby left for hours in a crib accumulates tensions she'll need to cry about and cry out as soon as she's in the presence of her primary contact figure.

When emotions are called up by suffering, lacking and frustration and can't be expressed right away, or remain unheard, they are physically inscribed in the body. As soon as the baby finds an opportunity to free herself of those tensions (maybe when her mother comes home in the evening) she makes the most of it and begins to sob. She is expressing distress and getting rid of the burden. She needs to be accompanied bodily and feel that what she is going through is respected. Then she can accept herself in her present emotional state without feeling threatened with destruction. It's counter-productive to try to stop the crying, whereas encouraging it enables the child to express and free herself of whatever is troubling her. The pediatrician T.B. Brazelton agrees with Aletha Solter about the need to discharge tensions accumulated tensions during the day. According to them most babies cry for at least an hour a day.

But be careful, when the baby cries, we may first of all attend:

*physiological* needs. Sometimes, the child is too cold or too warm or in need of a pee (and would prefer to do so without diapers). Scientists have also recently discovered that children who cry a lot have a species of intestinal bacteria (other those than those we all have) which provokes painful tummy ache, signaled but not discharged by crying.

*bonding* needs. A baby's basic needs – contact and food – are so fundamental that they are expressed via the level of the oxytocin (the hormone triggering and maintaining childbirth and lactation) secreted during the their satisfaction. And so on all through childhood and adult life. In this way, bonding and the associated pleasure are physiologically inscribed in the body

*exploration* needs. The baby is a human and, as such, is pushed by her innate curiosity and desire to try out her impact on the surrounding world. It's the opposite of constraint and concerns activation of the frontal lobes as she is the one who decides, moves and tests her power over things and people.

## My child cries for next to nothing

Later on, a toddler who whines and whimpers for next to nothing may be seeking a way of having a really good cry. If some feeling is blocked she will need to find a way of freeing herself of it, seeking permission or a pretext for giving vent to tears or anger. Even a child who can talk, or an adult, needs to cry, shout or stamp to get strong emotions out.

Nonetheless, there is real crying that heals and crying that prolongs the problem. Crying that serves no good purpose comes from the upper part of the chest and may be without tears. It is a substitute for crying and only helps repress rather than free emotions. Crying that liberates comes with sobs and tears. Holding the child tightly but tenderly against you will help until the penned-up emotion is freed. The child may resist and try to fight you off before being able to let out the sobs.

## Dreams and nightmares

Margot (at the age of five), came to see me in the middle of the night, "Mommy, I had a dream and I wanted to tell you about it. There was a wolf who caught a goat and shut it in a cage. I wanted to free it with my friends, but we were afraid of the wolf. I managed to open the cage. The goat came out but the wolf jumped on me and bit my hand."

All the characters in the dream can be looked at as if they were representing different parts of the dreamer.

We'd had a quarrel the day before. She had wanted me to tie a bow in her hair with a scarf. The result was a disappointment as it wasn't like her friend's, as she'd expected, and she got very angry. She shouted at me, hit me and wanted to throw my papers on the floor...

So what was the dream about? We can readily understand that a part of Margot's feelings (the goat) were shut up in a cage – that she was holding back her emotions. A goat is a stubborn creature with horns and knows what it wants. It could represent her desire. She managed (with her friends' help = with the pretext of the scarf) to free the goat. But she was afraid of the wolf, the personification of her aggressiveness. As soon as the goat was freed, the wolf jumped on her (as soon as she showed her emotion, her aggressiveness took over). She was afraid of what she had done and turned against herself, and the very hand that had hit her mommy was bitten by the wolf!

In another situation, when Margot was three, she found it difficult going to sleep at bedtime and sometimes woke up in the night, afraid of the wolf. We discovered that she regularly had that panic when she had hit her brother during the day.

When Margot hit her brother, she felt wicked. She didn't like that and projected the wicked part outside herself so that the wolf, not she, would be the bad one. But a wicked wolf is frightening and may punish the child for its wickedness. The underlying thought is, "I'm angry, but I'm not supposed to be. I'm wicked! No, the wolf's the wicked one and he's going to punish me. I'm scared!" Fear is often a way of turning unspeakable anger against onself. In fact, Margot was furious with her small brother, who got too much attention in her opinion. She needed her parents to reassure her about her importance in the family.

Wolves, monsters and ogres are all projections of the anger that must be rejected from ourselves to avoid destruction. A child may be afraid of the ogre under her bed, the monster in the cupboard or the wolf who's going to gobble her up when she's awake. She will also meet them in her sleep – as nightmares. All nightmares are to be taken seriously. By listening to our children, we get nearer them. We may try to understand together what the images mean and put words on their feelings. Talking about monsters already takes away a part of their power to frighten.

Monsters may be real life or TV images that haven't been understood and identified, shadows distorted by fear or the projection of unconscious emotions. We may look into what's going on in the daily context of family life or in the near past. If the nightmare is recurrent, then the more distant past must be explored.

Has the child been afraid of something in the past few days? Could she be angry about something? Is she missing out on something? Has there been cause for frustration? Is one of her parents absent? Have her parents had a dispute? Has she been hit? Is there some family secret that you didn't want or think to tell her about? Has she gone through something difficult: a loss, a worry, injustice, shock or a potentially traumatic events (hospital, a move, an accident…)? It sometimes happens that events from the distant past come to the surface months, or even years later. Emotions that have been pushed down often await some pretext to awaken and reappear in a dream in order to be taken into account.

Other than talking, drawing is an excellent means of coming to grips with nightmares, allowing a child to step back and feel she can master the situation. Drawing enables her to identify things, establish limits and fight her feeling of powerlessness, "I can look my nightmare in the face, put it onto a piece of paper and be stronger than it is. I have authority over it."

The following evenings, before going to bed, suggest your child does a drawing for all her worries "so they don't come and bother you during the night". Be careful not to interpret her drawing. Don't be tempted to get a psychological take on what is going on between her and herself. That doesn't mean not finding the root cause. Drawing is a useful technique for the first approach but, if the problem is important, it will not bring healing. The blocked emotion must always be freed.

If your child doesn't want to draw, or just so as to vary the range of possible solutions, you can invite her to imagine a 'worry box'. She can decorate it as she wishes in her mind's eye and, before going to sleep, she can put the worries of the day into it, close it tightly and only open it the next morning.

You can also give her some sort of doll or animal which can be her friend to share her worries with and in whom she can confide at bedtime. It's very important that the worries be met again and looked in the face in the morning or these techniques will cease to work. Worries must be listened to and solutions sought.

# 4

# The repression of emotions

"I'm not afraid" says Martin, boasting in front of his little girlfriend, but doesn't go near the worm she's holding.

"It doesn't even hurt" says Alexandra to her father who has just spanked her.

"I'm sorry"says Sarah to her little brother, repressing the immense anger she feels. A few minutes later, she bumps into a piece of furniture.

They are all denying what they feel, playing a part that is not theirs but a defence mechanism. They will lack deep-down security because they cannot trust what they feel inside. Just as Sarah bumped into the table, they will bump into the events in their lives.

Why did Sarah knock the table? It's a common everyday unconscious process. She felt an enormous hurt, having swallowed down her real feelings. In order to protect herself from that, she preferred to inflict another more physical, more objective hurt on herself, thus allowing her to feel and express pain. She wasn't allowed to cry over the humiliation she felt at having to apologize to her brother but she allowed herself to cry because she had got a bruise. And, of course, there will always be someone to say the judgemental, "You should be more careful!"

Whether the thoughts and feelings and behavior are pleasant or not, being able to recognize our emotions means accepting who we are and thus increasing our self-confidence.

Self-awareness is built little by little from different experiences on condition that the emotions are acknowledged, approved of and talked about. On the other hand, when those around them (parents, teachers etc.) systematically deny feelings, refuse to listen to or mock at emotions, children end up by thinking that what they think and do is not in conformity with what their parents expect of them.

Martin, Alexandra and Sarah's parents are probably proud of having such brave, strong or docile children, but they have no idea of the price that's being paid.

We all have our emotions and we all feel similar emotions in similar circumstances, since all human beings are physiologically 'wired' in much the same way. We have all, at some time, felt sad, fed up, afraid, scared stiff, furious, hateful, guilty, ashamed, excluded, jealous, envious, relieved or happy...

But since people speak so little of their deep feelings, each person feels she is the only one to feel what she feels and thinks she is different from others, with emotions that others don't know about. She often feels bad having such feelings, and thinks she is worthless, stupid or impossible... She passes negative judgements on herself and is worried that others think the same way. Consequently, she hides what she feels and puts on a mask, hoping it will correspond to what others expect of her. She is constantly anxious in case someone discovers that she's not who they think she is, so she tries to hide herself all the more.

We all have terrible fantasies, unpure thoughts or what we define as such because our parents weren't able to admit to having the same ones.

Our fantasies are mental images relating to a desire or an emotion. It may be one of absolute power in which I see my enemy tied to a post while I watch and laugh. It may be one of anger in which I see my enemy fall, be wounded, suffer... or a love fantasy where I see the boy I love come to get me on a dashing steed, or one of fear where I see a monster in pursuit, ready to devour me, or one of feeling despicable when I stand up to speak and people look at me condescendingly... There's no end to our fears and fantasies.

Who speaks about their fears, secret dreams or desires? Who mentions their loneliness, frustration, jealousy or even love and pleasure? Not so many people. So, not hearing about other's fears and inner life, we don't dare express ourselves. We soon come to the conclusion that emotions are unwelcome whether strange or unsuitable and we figure out it's safer to say nothing. It is often thought that the repression of urges is what makes life in society possible, and that if everybody expressed themselves freely, we wouldn't be able to live together. If we take a look at reality the degree of violence around us shows us that the repressive attitude is not the right one. Denial, non-consideration, non-realization of emotions does nothing but put them under pressure, ready to blow up when the safety valve gives way. It's true that if we give way to our impulse to hit, strangle, kill, torture each time we feel that way, then life would become impossible and would very rapidly disappear through generalized destruction. But is the repression of anger the only way of not killing one another? Isn't is possible to learn to acknowledge our feelings without them ruling our lives? Freud demonstrated that becoming aware of our destructive urges, far from making us de-structive, makes us con-structive. The desire to destroy and hurt is not an inherently human pulsion, but a mechanism to protect us from our emotions. So as not to feel that I hurt I may prefer to turn my rage against someone else. This repression in the unconscious mind can submerge the individual and lead him to act violently.

By acknowledging our feelings, accepting them, learning to live with them without fear of being destroyed, naming and talking about them we can remain aware of our whole being without acting anything out. It is important to show children that the *verbal* expression of their violent feelings and impulses destroys neither the relationship nor the person. We need to transmit, "I understand that you're angry and I love you just the same." If parents don't authorize the expression of their child's anger, she'll push it back, feeling guilty and worried. If her mother bursts out crying, she'll take on the worrying fantasy that she can destroy her mother. If she is beaten, she could be terrified at the idea of being destroyed, especially if she is very young and can't yet tell the difference between herself and another, perceiving the parent's violence as the natural continuation of her own.

When a child (and later the adult, if the childhood anguish hasn't been resolved) has to repress her rage she may be afraid of being destroyed from the inside. She will withhold the rage with determination, for if she lets it out, she will be afraid of exploding, literally falling to pieces! She is afraid of losing her physical boundaries, whereas the expression of her anger (which always has a real reason), would allow her to confirm them and assert her identity.

When parents remain insensitive to a child's emotion, sending her into her bedroom to cry to "get rid of her anger elsewhere", or when they don't pay attention to her, she is desperate. She has understood that her emotions threaten the relationship. She has practically no choice. She can't allow the bond to be broken as her survival is at stake. Her dependency is twofold, both for her primary needs of food and shelter and also for her deeper need of affection and connection. Consequently, in order to stay related, she must wipe out what she feels and become insensitive.

The psychologist Harold Bessell[3] uses another very strong image, *"When you work manually, your skin thickens to protect your hands and prevent blisters. When your emotions are rough-handled, something very like a corn forms to protect the tissues from future damage. It is neither so sensitive, soft or supple as the orignal skin. Someone covered in emotional corns is not able to perceive the outside world so fully or so adequately!"*

This is exactly what happens. We produce emotional corns in our childhood, which later alter our perception of the world and cause numerous problems. They protected us against upsurging emotions, and they now prevent us from being as aware as we might of what our children are experiencing. That's how we become 'thick-skinned'.

In order to accompany a child into self-awareness, the adult, if not completely devoid of psychic callouses, must at least be aware of them to put himself in the child's place without projection, and know her feelings without either filtering or interpreting them.

**Crying and sobbing, emotional expression, are the healing strategies of the body.** The problem is not to completely avoid being hurtful or unfair to the child. It so happens that we're not perfect! It's a question of allowing time and space for the emotional release of tensions he needs when he's been hurt.

## My baby wants her pacifier

Dummies that are are often given to babies in order to pacify them, meaning to stop or avoid them crying. They serve as tools for repressing emotions. When a baby cries, parents tend to think she wants a dummy to calm her down and go to sleep. In fact, it's the parents who can't stand to hear the baby crying, and they're asking her to be quiet, preventing her from freeing tension she will subsequently repress and push deep down inside.

Your baby is feeling an emotion, expressing a need and trying to tell you about it. It is true that a baby will use sucking and suckling to pacify herself. But if you give her something to suck, you're teaching her to need something in her mouth every time she experiences a difficult emotion. Later, isn't she likely to want to nibble something or chew her nails whenever she feels disturbed?

Moreover, recent studies showed that the use of a pacifier for a baby reduces her capacity for empathy. How come? Having a pacifier in the mouth during social interaction reduces face-muscle mobility implied in facial mimicry – smiling when the other smiles, express worry when the other looks worried. And it's this mimicry, as shown by studies on mirror neurons and links between emotion and motor skills, that helps a child integrate a panel of emotions he can identify and understand. This mimicking is at the origin of empathy, the ability to identify and feel what the other is feeling. Research has shown that when a pacifier was used regularly for five years, the facial mimicry at age seven were drastically reduced, becoming almost inexistant. Young adults tested at the age of nineteen who used a pacifier when they were babies had a notably low emotional intelligence.

## I've got a perfect baby who sleeps all the time

Haven't you heard that before? A lot of babies sleep so as not to cry. It's another way of cutting off unauthorized feelings. Sleep can also be a reaction to counteract stress.

I was amazed the first time I saw my baby doze off as soon as I took her into a shopping mall, but easily imagining what she felt, "Too much noise, to much tension... Help, I'm going to cut myself off!"

Babies need sleep sure enough! But sometimes, sleep is an escape.

## He's not very expressive!

Matthew never cries. He's never afraid of anything. He accepts frustration without saying a word. His family says he is brave and strong. He satisfies the social ideal of virility with the required 'stiff upper lip', and above all, he's not a nuisance. However Matthew is a human being, with human feelings and if he shows nothing, it's because he has already learnt to keep back his feelings, cover over his emotions and reduce his inner self to silence.

He may be imitating one or other of his parents, or even both. He may have suffered a real hardship, injustice, abandonment or loss he hasn't been able to express. He may feel it's dangerous to express what he feels. His emotions may have been systematically suppressed since he was tiny, or is it that his inner suffering is so intolerable that he prefers not to feel it. Whatever the situation, he needs help to come out of his shell and become truly alive. His self-denial is a measure of the suffering he is defending himself against.

Jason was very happy about the birth of his brother. At least, that's what his parents think. He's never shown any jealousy towards Martin, but always greeted him with pleasure, taking good care of him and, other than that, showing no change of behavior. His parents don't see that he has quite simply refused himself permission to feel any jealousy. He thought he was not allowed to, that he wasn't important enough, whereas by taking the role of the elder brother, he was sure of being noticed and accepted.

When her mother announced the divorce and her father's departure from home, Alison said nothing. She went to her bedroom, opened a book and started to read. Her mother felt relieved, feeling that Alison had accepted things very well. But how can you easily accept the separation of your parents? Only if there has been some form of violence or continual disputes. This wasn't the case of Alison's parents. In spite of differences and difficulties, they had maintained the image of a united couple. According to Alison's mother, she wasn't supposed to know that her parents didn't get on well.

What we often call 'taking it well', in fact means repressing feelings. Such repression is inevitably accompanied by some inner alteration, albeit invisible. Alison anesthetized herself. She felt nothing when her mother announced her father's departure, but she swore to herself never to fall in love and risk the suffering.

Pedro makes fun of his daughter, Amalia, who doesn't answer back. She doesn't get angry, because she knows her father would make fun of her susceptibility. Despite what her father says, "It doesn't mean anything", she is really hurt and the 'silly girl' and other invalidating comments resonate deep down and are received as being definitions of what she is.

Emotions are healthy and their repression endangers the sense of identity of the person. Children can hide their feelings, even to the extent of denying them completely. This is detrimental to their emotional and social abilities, lowering their emotional quotient.

To allow themselves to feel and express emotions children need their parents' permission and, in order for this to ensure its full value, it must be expressed both verbally and non-verbally. It must be manifested by the parents' real behavior and gestures of protection, one of the most important of which is to defend them from mockery. No one can express feelings if afraid of being exposed to ridicule and humiliation. To be able to trust an adult, a child must believe that the latter will protect him from possible mockery, and certainly not expose her to it.

To be able to really trust their parents, the child must also be sure of her parents' personal power. We're not talking about power as a constraining force to be wielded but as a feeling of inner certitude and ability to approve of one's own emotions. Showing oneself to be strong and hiding pain and fear from one's children does not reassure them but rather transmits the message that such dissimulation is how you should lead your life. Being powerful doesn't mean being insensitive but showing that you are not afraid of your feelings and are able to experience them freely and fully.

When we notice that our child is not showing the intensity of her feelings when facing a difficult situation, we may help her identify what she feels by naming the emotion and the possible cause, "You're furious because I didn't play as you wanted me to."

If parents are afraid of their emotions, the child may repress her own emotions and needs in order to protect her parents, as if unconsciously trying not to embarrass them. We can give her permission not assume that responsibility, "You're not responsible for your parents or for their emotions and feelings." Or, "You know I don't easily express my feelings and maybe you fear those emotions inside me. I can understand that, but no, don't go away or close yourself in. You may dare ask for what you need. I'll cope with my feelings. I'm the adult and can take care of myself."

## Does she sulk?

Sulking is a language. It announces suffering and isolation. The suffering is not understood, so the child prefers to ostensibly retire within herself.

Better avoid what would make it difficult for her to come out of his sulking with remarks like, "You're sulking!" or "When you've finished sulking, you can come and eat", which unnecessarily draw attention to the state of things. Saying or implying for instance something like, "I've no time for sulky children" is like saying, "I'm not interested in what's wrong for you."

There are a number of things you may do to unblock the situation,

**Try to find the emotion she's hiding with her sulks by formulating what you see she is feeling,** "I could see you weren't pleased when I told Joyce that..." Or "You're really angry when I don't give you ice-cream... "

**Help her to express her feelings**: "You have a right to say you're not pleased, you know!" Or: "If you feel it's not fair, you can tell him so. Do you think you're ready to tell him? How will you do that? Do you need help?"

**Show a certain indifference**, not of course ignoring the child but rather her closed-in behavior. Go on with your activities with her, taking care to reconnect. Indifference must be short-lived. And a child can't be left to sulk for more than two or three minutes or it would generate a vicious circle of more sulking and then it gets harder and harder for the child to come out unscathed.

**If she's little you can go to her and say tenderly,** "Honey, are you still upset?" Then take her in your arms and reconnect.

Invite her to do some new activity without referring to her sulks, answering the need for connection that lies behind the behavior, "Would you prefer we play outside together or roughhouse on the bed or bake some cookies?"

The problem must be addressed positively in a face-saving way, without the youngster feeling shameful. Humiliation is a psychological poison.

## Is she too nice?

She looks after her small brother or sister wonderfully well, without ever getting angry. If she seems too nice, she's probably refusing herself the right to be jealous, which she perceives as forbidden or dangerous via a mechanism that psychoanalysts call a "reaction scheme formation". Her behavior manifests the opposite of what she is really feeling. She is showing herself to be extra-nice so as not to let anyone see her not-niceness. She is unable to accept any aggressiveness or jealous feeling inside her, as she would feel bad, and that would be intolerable. Her niceness prevents contact with her hidden anger and reassures her that she is a 'nice little girl'.

It's helpful to give her permission to be jealous or angry, and say that these are natural feelings. She'll be pleased to hear about your own jealous feelings as a child. Unacknowledged jealousy in childhood alters relations with others later in life. When it is recognized and accepted, it can be overcome and healed.

## Does she accuse others?

Assuming the responsibility for doing something naughty or making some silly mistake is difficult and could make the child think she's mean and she most certainly doesn't want to be seen like that. She's nice, so the other one must be the bad one and so she throws the responsibility or inadmissible emotion is pushed onto a brother, a friend, some imaginary companion or even on you. Making her feel guilty would be counterproductive as the image she has of herself is already fragile and that's why she can't assume the emotion. You'll do a better job by helping her to consolidate a good image of herself and reassure her of your unconditional love and esteem, even when she makes a mistake, breaks a toy, knocks over a cup or hits her brother or sister...You can disapprove of her behavior but go on loving her in the same way as love is a fuel not a reward. You may reassure her that everybody feels rage or jealousy at times, can be careless, makes mistakes or, breaks things, hits or wants to hit people.

Many children between the ages of three and five invent imaginary friends to whom they attribute their 'naughty' behavior. Accusing them of lying would not be appropriate. It's their way of trying to cope with a surfeit of guilt. You could however, and with great respect, ask them to help their friend be more careful, thus putting the responsibility for the conduct back in their hands. Don't worry, children know their friends are make-believe even if they maintain the contrary. And, what is more, they know that you know that they know.

# 5
# Not repressing, but containing

Being truly interested in what children feel and think helps them to be themselves. Helping them into self-awareness means, first and foremost, really listening to them without judgement, without advice, without trying to guide, by simply letting them put words to what they're experiencing. Then they will be able to understand and accept their inner feelings.

Our adult's brain has matured, allowing us the possibility of managing emotions on our own. A child's brain hasn't finished its development. The frontal lobes devoted to monitoring anticipation, empathy and focusing on others, as well as the superior cortical regions which enable us to relativise emotions, put things into perspective with words and find meaning, are still under construction. The limbic region is responsible for feeling fear, laughter or tears without mediation from the more evolved zones. Children need adults to help them cope with such difficult feelings, canalize their energy and learn how to express their needs in a socially acceptable way, knowing that they are not at risk when they express what they feel. Consequently, they must not be left alone with their raw emotions when they don't have the mental equipment to manage the depth of what they are experiencing. It would be leaving them unarmed to face the whole battery of archaïc defence mechanisms such as denial, cancelling, psychological cleavage, projection and reaction formation, which are efficient means of avoiding feeling (the 'corns' we met above), but with serious alteration in the possibility of contacting reality.

Rather than leaving our children alone to cope with with their inner monsters, we can be there with them. Parents have the responsibilty of their children's emotional security. If we feel wounded when Martin hits us saying, "I don't love you any more", and if we listen to our hurt rather than his, our reply could be, "I don't love you either" or "Go to your room and don't come back till you've calmed down" and Martin would feel terribly abandoned. If he hits us and shouts at us it's because he's seeking contact. We can't allow ourselves to reject him because we are the ones he needs. A child is a child and hasn't quite learnt how to say things properly. Parents should be there to help find the right words rather than going into emotional competition. An adult has the means of controlling his emotions. It's in the order of things that children's emotions should take priority over those of their parents. It's certain that as children grow older the parents' role recedes. But if they are left alone into their emotional jungle too early, they're deprived of guidance and left to their uncoached defence devices to control their anguish.

To better understand what's going on, let's have a look at a small baby. As she is very young, she has no individual awareness of herself as a subject separate from her mother. We, as adults, know that we *have* a feeling of hurt and that we exist outside it. A baby, first of all, *is* hurt, invaded by her distress and desperately needing her mother to help. She needs her voice, her smell, her love – to be enveloped in her presence! As her mental and physical boundaries are ill-defined as yet, the contact with her mother is what enables her to contain her feelings and feel reassured and whole.

Children live in the present moment as they haven't finished developing their capacity to project into the future, and the intensity of what they are experiencing is inevitably greater. They don't know that their suffering will cease, that their anger will go away and that they will be able to find their proper comfort again while they are busy struggling with their emotions. We, as adults, know that the present will pass. A child needs the complete support of her parents when assailed by an emotion. She also needs to experiment that her emotions don't have the power to destroy neither her nor her parents.

What do you think? Should we take a crying baby into our arms or let her cry for fear of spoiling her?

## Should we attend to the slightest cry?

A newborn baby will cry. She's hungry. If her mother responds within ninety seconds, it takes five for her to calm down. If she responds after as long as three minutes, she'll take fifty seconds to calm down. So, when the waiting time is twice as long the crying time is ten times longer. The longer you wait, the more difficult it is for her to re-organize and re-harmonize herself.

What happens for her if the person doesn't come? She has no way of saying, "It'll pass over". She *is* absolute pain. She has no means of saying that her mother will come sooner or later, when she's finished the washing-up, phoning or whatever else she might be doing. She exists as hurt... and nobody comes. Her mother who should help and protect her is not there to do that, which means that she is capable of hurting her! She must be dangerous and can't be trusted. That's impossible! How can you lose trust in your mother, the one who you depend on for your survival? So, the baby maintains trust in her mother and opts for an alteration of her inner perception finally cancelling her suffering and emotions because they're too dangerous. Her dependency on her mother increases, because she has lost her own landmarks, and her mother remains the one who knows *what* is needed and *when*, playing the role of absolute authority.

On the other hand if parents show their children love, whatever emotions are shown, the baby will learn that they're not dangerous, be ready to listen to them and learn to recognoze what they're telling him, because her parents are there to listen. This is what allows a child to build up an idea of her **permanence**. Whether sad, happy or angry, she is the same child, the same being.

## What should we do?

When a child feels emotion, your question very likely is, "How can I help her become aware of what is going on inside?"

A newborn baby needs to be attended to as soon as possible. Our job is there, trying to find out what's wrong and satisfying the need. The baby knows better than any doctor or clock when she's hungry. We have to be there for her when she expresses what she feels, whatever it may be. If all her physiological needs are satisfied and the crying continues, then there must be some psychological need.

Staying near, keeping eye contact and listening with our heart, will enable her to confide her distress or protestation.

The older a child gets, the more independent she becomes in dealing with her emotions. You may take a few minutes before rushing to see how she's coping. If she doesn't ask for anything, then trust her. She simply needs time and space to express herself. We have a tendancy to want to console. I feel it strongly in myself, but I hold back. When one of my children cries, I try to listen before I try to console, "I can see you've hurt yourself!" If she's hurt herself badly, I encourage her to cry, "You cry, honey, hold on to me and cry because it really hurts."

The question 'why' is to be avoided. "Why are you crying?" can be received as an accusation or humiliation and can be heard as suggesting there's no good reason. Such a question means thinking it over and the child isn't there yet. She first needs to express her emotion before talking about it. Moreover, knowing why she's crying would tempt us to want to solve the problem and give solutions. That's not what she needs. She's most likely quite capable of dealing with her problem all on her own, if only her emotion can be heard.

Instead of 'why' questions, you may try asking, "What's happening?" or "What are you feeling inside your heart?" which are ways of going along with the child's inner feelings.

## Listening with empathy

Listening with empathy involves thinking about what you're actually hearing in what the child is saying, by holding onto the meaningful aspects, which are the emotions, feelings or wishes. It's not so much listening to the words as understanding what they imply.

Concentrate on the inner feelings rather than on the facts announced. Accompany your child, not the outside events.

When we hear, "I don't want to go to sleep!" We could reply, "Oh, so you really don't want to?" rather than, "You need your sleep so as not to be tired tomorrow. " We can go on by saying something like, "I can quite understand you not wanting to, you're having so much fun playing. (And all the while, getting her ready for bed.) Maybe you don't believe it, so why not try it out!

If you are already into power games with your children, it's very likely that in the first days you'll come up against some resistance. Is it so very terrible if they go to bed a bit late? Learning how to respect your own rhythms is worth twisting a few rules. When they understand that you respect their feelings without going into a power game, they will accept feeling their tiredness and go to bed more easily and at the right time for them. We can often trust our children to know what's good for them unless we're trying to prove we're the strongest which is, unfortunately, very often the case.

We have to be aware that the way we reformulate what's going on – our deep-down attitude – is more important than the words we pronounce. A beautiful, well-phrased sentence catching the child's precise experience can be utterly useless. It's a question of going along with and being in EMPATHY, and that involves capturing the emotional resonance beyond the actual words, putting yourself in her shoes, feeling what she feels. It means listening to her from inside.

"Mommy, am I going to tennis or going to do my homework?"

"You're hesitating. What do you think feel like doing feel like doing?"

"I don't want to do the maths test."

"You seem worried."

By reformulating, we are not judging, we are not commenting, we're not interfering. We're just accepting what is being said. Then the child feels confirmed and can allow herself to experience, express and trust her feelings. It's incredible how much good this attitude will bring – to her, to us and to our relationship. We have to be careful to respect our innermost feelings. Of course, it's important not to force her to say something. As in all things, excess is counterproductive. Reformulating systematically and permanently could very well have the opposite effect and make our children aggressive to protect themselves from such constant intrusion, or possibly make them too dependent on our attention. We can trust our children. Our role is not to smooth out difficulties and resolve their problems – they don't need us for that but they do need us to help them find their own confidence and resources, ready to face whatever situation crops up.

Beware of thought-reading and interpretation. Our own repressed emotions from way back can color our empathy and be projected on the child. Emotional decoding must remain respectful of her different shades of feeling. Interpreting because of what we feel and thinking for her would, once more, be limiting her to a given definition of herself, which would be quite the opposite of truly listening to her.

In conclusion, the way of accompanying a child's or anyone else's emotions is simply a question of compassion, trying to feel what the person feels in the same position and the same circumstances. Nothing human is foreign to a human. We've been a child too and can understand what is going on behind the lines.

And also beware of getting involved with possible 'psychological' angles. Sometimes it's not necessary to put things into words and, on the other hand, it may not be enough. Physical contact and cuddling is always a good response and satisfies a fundamental need for connection. It's not a question of trying to put words to a child's behavior but rather helping her find those necessary. Basically, that means helping her to get out of a situation apparently without issue or accompanying a painful event.

## Steps for emotional coaching

Be present in an attitude of acceptance, with eye contact, breathing and openness. A young child will be best in our arms.
Name the child's feeling and the cause, "I can see that you're angry/sad/frightened, because when…"
Allow the emotion to flow.
Only when breathing is back to normal can words come out and can we discuss the situation.

Of course, such listening in empathy is likely to bring you up against your own emotions, lacks and distress from your own past, the things you missed out on…

It's difficult to respect a child's anger when we don't know how to be healthily angry ourselves. It's practically impossible to take a child in your arms when she's sad if this reminds us too strongly of distress our parents were never able to accompany.

Essentially, if our children cannot reveal their inner truth to us, once they become adults they may end up by turning away, even cutting themselves off from us. Or, maimed in some way, their wings injured, they may be unable to fly away from home.

So many parents don't understand why their children, as adults, cease coming to see them when they've 'done everything' for them. Everything but respect their feelings.

# 6

# She gets on my nerves with her whining

Sometimes you find your children's emotions exasperating. There are several possible reasons for this:

You're quite simply worn out and emotions tend to be noisy.

You have your own emotions and needs that are not being acknowledged and this puts you in competition with your child.

The emotional reaction expressed is not a genuine motion but a screen hiding your real feeling.

It's an emotion you don't allow yourself.

It reminds you of your own childhood.

## Too much is too much! When things get out of hand

When a small child cries 'for nothing', she's probably tired. It's the same for adults, so when parents get angry 'for nothing' (choosing this mode of expression more often than tears) they're very probably just tired.

Too many parents refuse to acknowledge that they're worn out. They want to give more and more, do the washing up, the laundry and cleaning, tell a story, play with Barbie dolls and be 'good parents'. Sooner or later they blow up for as little as an upset cup or a pair of pants trailing on the floor.

Acknowledging our tiredness and letting the children know how we're feeling can help them understand the real reason for us being so cross. It's not that they're really unbearable but that our limits have been reached at that particular moment. We are not able to stand noise and disorder so well, and we need some peace and quiet.

## When one emotion hides another

You are exasperated when Martha bursts into tears because her skirt is too tight, when Oliver is terrified by his grand-mother's perfectly inoffensive dog or when Peter gets angry with his brother for next to nothing.

Listen to your intuition will help you understand what's going on beneath the surface. You're facing and reacting to an emotional distortion. Martha's real emotion is anger. Oliver's fear is at having to leave his mother for a few days. He's afraid she might not come back to get him and doesn't dare say so. Peter is anxious scared about his math test. Your own exasperation shows you that there's another, more crucial problem to be listened to.

When emotions can't be told directly, they may can get shifted onto other objects (a piece of clothing, a dog, a snail, someone else) when math is the real problem. They can be used to hide the truth and disguise the real need that cannot be voiced

## Do as I do...

How can you stand your daughter howling in anger when you were never allowed to say 'no' to your own mother? How can you accept your son crying when you've never shed a tear?

A father who doesn't show his emotions will expect his sons to be 'strong', like him. A mother who doesn't express what she feels will find it difficult to to cope with her daughter's tantrums.

Do you we forbid emotions in your children? We were forbidden them by our own parents, or we repressed them because they were too dangerous. Accepting to hear them in our son or daughter would be going against unconscious decisions taken in our own early childhood. It would oblige us to question the upbringing we received and we may not want to hear our inner child so as to protect the image we have of our own parents.

## She's not supposed to be angry because you're the one that is!

Your toddler wants his pasta with tomato sauce and we give him butter... and he yells. Your teenage son is ranting and raging about his history teacher. Your daughter screams at her brother because he's playing his music as loudly as possible. You're usually pretty patient, but today you're NOT. You're beside yourself.

For some reason you're angry. You silently reproach your husband because he is quietly reading his newspaper and leaving you to do everything. Or you are angry with your

114

wife who's sulking, or your boss, the plumber, your mother – and your child is the one who's furious. It's the last straw. You blame the child and blow your top!

So he doesn't like his pasta? Your problems are so much more important than a silly grouching about tomato sauce, history teacher or noisy music!

It's amazing to see how many of our emotions remain unknown to us. They come out via the exasperation we feel with our children though, we must admit, they make us mad. Is it quite by chance that they are particularly annoying just when we are feeling ruffled? It's as if they're looking for trouble? Yes of course, children are extremely sensitive to their parents' emotional climates. By some form of telepathy they capture unspoken words and tensions and, feeling insecure, they react with behavior which will provoke their parents' exasperation until the tension is freed.

"You would think that they're making me yell at them on purpose!" exclaims Vicky.

The less aware of their emotions parents are, the more their children will express them by proxy. They manage to push their parents 'over the edge' and get them to express something.

Have you never felt extremely annoyed by some wish or behavior of your child? Have you never been unable to stand your baby's crying, your teenage son's anger or your eldest daughter's despair? Have you never insulted them without being able to hold yourself back?

We may ask ourselves the following questions: "For what reason could I be feeling angry at this precise moment?" Is there some lack, frustration or feeling of being powerless? Have I been hurt? Have I a difficult problem to sort out?

115

## When she does that, I lose control!

It's when our children remind us of our own childhood that we are least able to keep our temper.

"Eat your soup!" shouts Vanessa. Roy pushes the dish away and it overturns, splashing soup all over the kitchen and on his mother, who loses her temper. She seizes him by the arm, gives him a slap and calls him a 'naughty boy'. Vanessa admitted to me later on, "I felt my own mother's violence take hold of me." So, what happened that day? Usually her son eats up without any difficulty, but that day, Vanessa's nerves were seriously frayed. Roy felt her stress and, as children will, lent himself to her emotional needs, giving her the opportunity to relieve herself of her anger and get rid of it.

Vanessa had indeed felt herself being taken over by an uncontrollable fury. She was reliving her mother's violence, but this time she was not on the receiving end. As a child, she had often been the victim and, as an adult, she took on the role of persecutor, with Roy duly cast in that of the victim. Her mother had never been able to stand any disobedience, would easily become violent and hit her daughter.

Paula has a two and a half year-old son. After the first few minutes in the park she's fed up, although she feels guilty at not enjoying it, and goes every Thursday afternoon. She has taken a day off every week to be with her son and devotes all her evenings and weekends to him. She spends as much time with him as she can and blames herself for feeling boredom.

Why does she get bored? Boredom means repressed emotions and her boredom allows her not to feel them.

116

What is the nature of her repressed feelings and where do they come from?

Paula's parents never played with her. She doesn't remember any moments of closeness and pleasure with either of her parents. She refuses to see how much she suffered. She said that that was the way it was... Because of that denial of her emotions as a little girl she finds herself unable to play and laugh with her son.

In order to compensate she does everything for him, everything that's she thinks is good for him and she thinks will make him happy. She takes him to the park so he can ride on the poneys and merry-go-rounds but represses her emotions and won't listen to her own frustration. When she gets home her unconscious rage guides her towards some form of destruction. She absentmindedly puts her favorite cashmire pullover into the washing-machine and finds it shrunk and matted when she takes it out – she's managed to punish herself! She was feeling guilty and found this way of turning the aggressiveness against herself and authorizing her feelings of guilt, by paying the price.

All parents relive their own childhood via their children. And that's the source of many a problem. Projections of their own experience, the surfacing of repressed feelings of hate and jealousy, family secrets, memories of humiliation, frustration, shame and guilt. All our past experiences are there, mostly unconscious, and prevent us from behaving appropriately with our own children.

**When the past hasn't been healed, parents automatically, instinctively reproduce their own parents' behavior.**

Repetition of abusive and violent behavior is a way of shelving difficulty and pain to the extent of denying it, like saying, "I do as my mother or father did because it was good for me, it did me no harm." It's a complex mechanism. Identifying with an abusive parent is an unconscious way of trying to understand what was going on for them, as well as being a way of seeking revenge for the suffering experienced, a way of allowing the intense rage to at last find expression, however misplaced. Revenge is taken on some substitute figure, maybe one's own child, maybe some vulnerable or dependent person or an animal. As these people are innocent, the need for revenge is insatiable.

When our conscious mind is aware of having been traumatized, we often try to do the very opposite for our children but, despite this, we obtain the same results. And anyway, the opposite is just a question of two sides of the same coin. Doing the opposite is another way of refering to what our parents did, and still not managing to be in contact with our own children.

## Healing our own childhood

The only way of really being able to listen to our children is by healing our own difficult childhood experiences. In order to free ourselves from the past, we need to be able to let go of our emotions. Our parents weren't able to pay attention to our emotional needs or listen to our fears and angers. The wounds inflicted stay stamped on us because we have not been able to cry them out. We often haven't even been able to identify the hurt and injustice, as we were always told us it was *for our own good*. No witness was there to establish the truth. We've pushed down our tensions and now they're coming to the surface with our children.

To be able to heal, it's necessary to look the reality of our own childhood in the face. It's time to cease idealizing our parents and dare to see what was wrong, hurtful or unfair. Remembering the past means allowing ourselves to feel the emotions to which we didn't have access as children. When we've expressed our anger and cried with compassion over the child we were, we'll be able to see our children in their true light.

Do they bring to the surface feelings you can't stand? That's where there's an emotional knot. We can learn to face it by just letting the memories mount to the surface. Let's listen to the child in us, what she never received – someone who cared about her feelings. Find the images of the little boy or girl we were and open up a place in our heart where they're welcome.

In our present adult mind we can imagine that we are going to go back to being the child we once were. It's helpful to imagine a meeting between the self of today and the one of the past and then let the adult of the present cuddle the child of the past, listen, understand and love him or her.

To help you do this sort of work you may wish to be accompanied by a psychotherapist or listen to a cassette of guided relaxation that will help you bring memories to the surface and allow you to heal them.

# Chapter IV

## Fear

Queuing for the big wheel, an eight-year-old girl was crying, "I don't want to go, I'm scared!"

"It's not dangerous, don't be such a coward? You're not going to spoil our day!"

The little girl cries all the harder. A woman in the queue intervenes, saying, "It's OK to be afraid. There's no need to spoil your pleasure. Go ahead and let her wait for you. I'll look after her." The little girl breaks out in a wide smile. She's been listened to. The other members of her family get in the nacelle and she stays on the ground watching and finds another little girl to chat with. She's radiant.

Obliging children to confront a problem is useless and only increases their fear. Helping someone to get past fear takes time, time for wanting to stop feeling afraid and take up another stand. When the decision comes from you the child is obeying your choice not his, and is not using his own resources. Being dependent in this way increases fear.

# 1
## Should we listen to his fears?

On the beach Thomas, just two, is petrified. He refuses to go into the water even with nice duck water-wings. His father has also bought a dinghy but Thomas screams when he tries to lift him in.

His parents are thrilled at the idea of being able to splash around with their little boy and have bought him all sorts of colored toys – and there he is, terrorized at the idea of dipping his toes in the water or trusting such an unstable object as the dinghy. Sometimes small children find it difficult to understand what makes their parents put them in such unpleasant situations.

And it's so frustrating for the parents! Vexatious for some, who can't stand the idea that their offspring are not up to their expectations. They don't understand because last year he loved water! And they may become aggressive, looking enviously at those parents whose children are diving, jumping in and otherwise happily splashing about. Some parents don't measure how great their children's fear can be, think them ridiculous and throw them in the water regardless of their cries.

Why not take the time? Why not let children get used to this strange element, water, at their own rhythm. Is it to show other parents that their child can swim or so as not to have a child who could be seen as a coward? Forcing a child into doing something is not the best way of helping him overcome his fears and could have unfortunate consequences later on.

A parent might be proud to say, "My son's not afraid of anything" but a child who denies all fear may be in fact so afraid of his own fear that he prefers not to feel it, pushing it down into his unconscious mind. It will come out sooner or later in life, in a more or less disguised or misplaced way. It's natural and normal that children should feel fear and it's important that we, as adults, don't incite them to be *too* brave.

Alan bites his nails. At night he snores and twitches during his sleep. He doesn't see that as a sign of worry. He thinks that that's just the way he is. He doesn't feel fear. He likes dangerous sports, adventurous trips to countries at war and thrillers. He flirts with fear but doesn't feel it. In most situations where people are afraid, he's quite at ease –but he bites his nails!

Years later, at the age of forty, he started to seek therapy and was then to find out what prompted that behavior. He discovered his fear, a most surprising fear. It didn't fit in with his self-image. When he accepted this new version of himself, he remembered the absence of attention from his parents, the distress he felt faced with their lack of dialogue and his immense loneliness as a little boy. Taken aback by the terror that surged up, he became aware that he had so much fear inside that he had preferred not to feel it. With all fear abolished, he needed not only sensational activities to make him feel his very existence but also to constantly test the control he could exercise over his fear. It was his deep-down unconscious fear that called him to confront all possible dangers.

After allowing himself to feel and then to express the terror that had been there since childhood, he was able to free himself of it. To his wife's great relief his twitching ceased as well as his snoring – both witness to his enormous emotional repression - and his breathing at night also calmed down.

**Children whose fears are systematically mocked never become open and brave adults**. They may well deny all fear and display great temerity, tending to take bigger and bigger risks in order to feel something and prove how much control they have over themselves. But they may stay shy and retiring all their lives, dependent on anti-depressants or more illicit drugs to counteract anguish and fears that remain unspeakable and difficult to overcome.

They may find it difficult to trust other people enough to engage a relationship and share intimacy. How can you trust others when your parents have shown such insensitivity. Being dependent on someone is felt to be fraught with danger. How can you dare to love?

Other people, especially if anger has been forbidden them, may build up defenses by developing phobies. These limit fear, focalizing on a particular object, which may or may not be at the origin of the fear. It could be the water they were thrown into, the dark cupboard or cellar they've been threatened with or even locked up in. It could shift to something else, for instance elevators, means of transportation, cats, spiders, snakes…

People with fears that are laughed away, denied, stifled with drugs, projected outside or terribly invasive indicate that, as children, their fears were ignored to the extent that they now have a disturbed attitude concerning that emotion.

Thus, fear is not there by chance even if the reason remains obscure for the adults we are. Fear is to be respected, listened to and accepted. A brave person is not the one that that feels no fear but someone who knows all about it, who can admit it and learn from it. Feeling no fear is dangerous since this fundamentally healthy emotion informs us of danger and prepares our bodies and minds to face it in the unknown world around us. Fear is natural, to be lived through and used.

Having said this, there are also disproportionate fears and those that miss the mark, inhibit, paralyze and are of no practical use. However, they are there to be listened to and taken into account as messages. They are saying something about your child or your child is trying to say something in this way.

There are healthy fears, but also inappropriate fears. Some are to be gone through, some to be gotten over, but all are to be respected and accompanied.

# 2

# The most frequent fears

There are different sorts of typical fears that most human beings go through during their childhood. They can concern the fear of, falling, loud noises, unknown faces, separation (chapter IX, Life is not a bed of roses), the bath, water in their eyes, the dark, animals, wolves, ghosts, witches, dragons and other strange creatures... Fears can appear and disappear. They reflect the developmental stages of a child's psyche. Normal at certain ages, they only become problematical if they intrude too much on the child's life or last too long.

We'll explore some of the more frequent fears.

## Loud noises

A loud noise makes us jump. For a small child, it can lead to real panic. It seems to me that this belongs to archaïc reflexes destined to protect the species. Noise signals a potential danger which indicates flight, but of course a baby can't flee on his own, he can only howl.

Lucy is twenty months old. There are works and bricks in the next-door, semi-detached house. Suddenly the noise starts up deafeningly! It sounds like a jackhammer and the wall shudders. The noise terrorizes the little girl, who howls, thrashes about and sobs.

Her mother takes her in her arms and quickly goes away. In a quiet environment, she hugs her daughter and tenderly lets her sob her heart out. Echoing the rhythm of her daughter's breathing, she whispers softly, "You've been so frightened. The noise was really loud, I felt frightened too (it was true). It makes you afraid when you don't expect it, and then suddenly 'brououou'! It makes you wonder what's going on. Do you know what made that noise?"

"No", replies the little girl between hiccups.

"Do you want to see what it was?"

"No."

Her mother is just a bit too prompt in introducing Lucy to the source of the terrible noise – she's still too frightened. So she talks about the works next door and explains what the builders are doing and how the vibrations affects their house too.

As the work will last for two weeks, and it's not possible to be out of the house all day, it's important to give Lucy the means to face the stress. She and her mommy practice shouting at the wall behind which the builders were working, "Stop that noise! It's driving us mad!" Of course, that doesn't alter the noise, but it changes how Lucy feels about it. Expressing anger and being forceful is the best way of diminishing fear. For nearly a month after the works, Lucy remained attentive to all the sounds around her. If a dog barked nearby she would say, "The dog frightened me." She was not needing a reply other than an acknowledgement, "Yes, you were afraid of the noise."

Talking at length about the noise and the fear it was causing was the best way of comforting and reassuring her daughter.

It helped make her feel whole again and able to cope with her emotion.

## Fear of going to sleep

Light from the streetlamps filters through the shutters and makes moving patches on the wallpaper because the wind is blowing the leaves on the trees outside. Such shadows can be really terrifying for a child who doesn't know what's going on. The father takes the little boy in his arms, opens the shutters and watches the branches waving about outside for a long time. Then he shuts them and the two watch the shadows dancing on the wall. He lies down next to his son, who goes straight to sleep.

We need to feel safe to be able to go to sleep. Getting up to see a child when he cries out in the night is what gives him that feeling, and he will know that he can count on his parents. A nightlight can be left to enable him to distinguish things in the dark if he wakes up in the middle of the night but cannot replace the presence of a parent.

Sleep means letting go, releasing control and slipping into another world, dreaming dreams or perhaps nightmares. We like to be accompanied.

After the bedtime story, a massage can bring a feeling of security and ensure a peaceful night's sleep. Being touched and stroked brings a feeling of being contained. It's reassuring to feel our body contours.

Bedtime is a very special moment for talking about the events of the day, a moment for rounding off some unfinished event, answering questions left in suspense or talking about a worry. Are there nightmares? Is there some object that changes into something else during the night? Does his nightlight make a threatening shadow?

It's worth paying attention. Maybe he's just saying he needs you nearby. He's not being capricious, he's expressing a need. By lying down next to him for a while, you give him a feeling of security that will stay with him all his life. By refusing to satisfy his demand, you would be obliging him to face darkness and venture into the unknown world of sleep all alone. He will of course learn how to go to sleep all on his own, but at the price of spending emotional energy which won't be available for other apprenticeships. The anguish of repressed fears may well be at the bottom of much backwardness in the acquisition of language, elocution or the pronunciation of certain syllables.

Night terrors that wake up the child speak of badly managed daytime emotions.

## Should we be wary of fairy stories?

Margot, at two and a half, woke up in the middle of the night, screaming that she was afraid of the wolf. I discovered that, just the day before, her grandmother had given her a book about the wolf that tried to eat the little goat kids. We talked it over. I explained the story very slowly, retracing everything and going back over things. Then I said I didn't like this story that was making her frightened. So, what should we do with the book? I suggested four options: keeping it, burning it, tearing it up or throwing it away. She thought about it and then said very decidedly, "We'll tear it up", which she conscientiously proceeded to do, saying, "There, I've torn up the book so the wolf can't eat the little goats."

Traditional tales are often violent. They're the remains of a period of history when people told children stories to frighten them into obedience and submission. If you listen to old lullabies, you'll get a good idea of the family atmosphere reigning in many families where the bedtime message would be, "Go to sleep or the bogeyman will come and get you." This seems particularly true in France, where many lullabies were threatening. We find wolves, monsters and other witches all over the place. Some psychoanalysts who've analyzed their symbolic meanings and noted their universality have warned against fairy tales. It's true they carry symbols but if left unexplained they don't help to heal and may even serve to repress emotions, projected on the symbols and thus shelved and avoided. I share the opinion of Alice Miller[4] in thinking that symbols help to keep things on the unconscious level. Cathartic healing does not come via symbolization, otherwise artists would be relieved of their hurt by their art. Painting, writing, sculpture and all art-forms help them to survive by maintaining their emotional repression. On the other hand, it's possible to look at a painting as one would listen to a dream and put colors and shapes on the canvas to explore an emotional pathway.

Art-therapy is a very powerful therapeutic tool, where sculpture, painting, collage etc, are mediators, and in which the person is in dialogue with himself. His unconscious mind finds expression in an art-form. Such symbols are meaningful because they are an expression of the unconscious mind. Words are healing because they give life to feelings. They enable us to describe what is going on in our minds, find greater awareness and structure our intimate experience.

Unfortunately, reading a fairy tale rarely brings awareness. Tales from times gone by certainly carry images of the psyche, but are they good for our children? I think not. My clinical experience leads me to think that they can be harmful. A child who's going through difficulties treated in the tale can find his negative beliefs confirmed, and remain with his fears. Such tales depict unconscious fantasies that are likely to re-enforce fear and anguish.

Julia was afraid of Snow-White's stepmother for years. She was so terrified that she tried to hide the book. Her brother would knowingly open the book in front of her at the page where she becomes a wicked witch, just to see his sister shudder. In fact, Julia was afraid of her own mother and, at the unconscious stage, had felt much anger against this woman who behaved like a witch. She had idealized her mother for a long time, refusing to feel her real emotions. It was if she had lived in a forest far away from her castle, in exile from herself. A Prince Charming had taken her far from her mother until she did psychotherapy and eventually found and dared express her feelings, having regained her self-confidence.

Rosalda had a problem of incest with her father. She went five times to see the French film *Peau d'Âne* (*Donkey Skin*, made after the traditional fairy tale written by Charles Perrault and first published in 1694), feeling confusedly that this tale concerned her but without finding any particular resource. It's a story, better known in the French than in the Anglo-Saxon world where a King seeks to marry his daughter. To escape this terrible destiny, she names a number of impossible requests (gowns the color of the sun the moon and the stars and fine enough to pass through a ring and a donkey skin producing jewels) to avoid the incestuous marriage. Her father accomplishes these impossible tasks but she finally escapes in the donkey skin and, after a ritual adventure, ends up marrying her Prince.

For years, Thelma had been afraid of finding herself alone in the cold like the *Little Match Girl*. So as not to be rejected she complied with other people's desires, quite forgetting to be herself. Now over fifty, she still cries over that story.

How is it that *Bambi, Cinderella, Hansel and Gretel* are all stories in which parents die (especially the mothers) or otherwise abandon their children? We may note in passing that all these stories are written by men. Is it, for them, a way of saying how difficult it was to leave their mothers?

There is one other interpretation – they had mothers that were hard, tyrannical and unkind, but like all children, dreamt of a sweet, loving mother. Anger against their real mother was out of the question, and so they would need to permanently idealize her, unable to give up that image. A timely death would thus safeguard her good image and the pent-up inexpressible anger can be projected onto the wicked witch who tortures and abuses. It's easy to kill a witch without feeling guilty! The message is clear, the child hasn't the right to feel anger against his mother. These stories tell of an even deeper powerless rage. Many such stories are told in order to support a strict and authoritative education and thus protect an idealized image of the parents, completely deforming reality in a morally unjustifiable way.

In what way can this sort of story help a child build his character? Why give images that can be terrifying?

Why not leave children the choice of their own symbols? There's no denying that those who receive these stories in a painfully dramatic way are those with a similar underlying problem. But what purpose do these tales serve? Why not choose present-day stories? There are so many excellent ones.

## Do children like feeling frightened?

Some say yes, that fear exerts a sort of fascination but that doesn't mean that children really *like* what makes them feel fear.

A science-fiction film is being shown in the plane taking us to our vacation destination. My two-year old son, Adrian, sits up in his seat to watch and murmurs, "I don't like that monster, I don't want to see it." I try to have him sit down, which would be enough to take the film out of his visual field, but it's impossible. He's fascinated. I turn round and see four-year old Margot also standing up, completely hypnotized by the giant hydra writhing on the screen. They haven't stood up at any other time and don't even have earphones to hear the sound. They're just bewitched by the weird picture.

When we're frightened we need to negotiate the emotion and understand what's happening. To feel reassured, it's better to face the cause, identify and come to terms with the problem. Adrian talked about the hydra, "I didn't want it. It was wicked." And yet, at the time, he couldn't take his eyes off it. Unfortunately, the next day Adrian was given a book about Hercules, signed Walt Disney. It was another story about monsters, including a hydra very much like the one on the screen!

Adrian wanted to look at the book over and over again. Did he enjoy the pages with the monsters? In fact, he needed to see them to reassure himself and take control over them. He began having nightmares until I pinned down the culprit. I invited Adrian to draw his nightmare and I took away the book until he was old enough to look at a monster without being afraid. The nightmares stopped immediately.

## The dragon that lives in tunnels

The following Summer, we went to visit some caves.

"No, I don't want to go, I don't want to see the dragon", said Adrian, clutching on to me desperately. Although a few minutes ago he had been excited at the idea of the visit, when the door opened on the dark cave, he refused to go in. In the cave there was a dragon, obviously! He was terrified and hung onto me. I went in with Adrian in my arms and talking to him all the time. A cocoon of reassuring words helps a child to feel safe. A bit later, having seen that there was no dragon in the cave, he became angry, "I don't want the dragon! I don't want the cave, I don't like it!"

This incident enabled me to identify the origin of his fear of tunnels. A month earlier, we had gone to Disneyland. There was a cave with an articulated dragon that moved its head about and breathed out smoke. It was so true to life that Adrian had thought it was alive. In spite of my efforts to show him the mechanisms he remained convinced that the monster was real. At the time, I admit that I hadn't realized the importance of this. Adrian wanted to go back and see the dragon and, to avoid his being frightened, I preferred not to take him. There were so many other things to see! However, from that day on he started to be afraid of going through tunnels in the car. As soon as he went in, he would cry, "Let me out! I don't want to be trapped inside, I don't want to be in the tunnel!"

"What don't you like about it?"

"There are dragons. I don't like dragons."

Faced with the fact that it was impossible to make him understand that the dragons were not real, I tried another angle, helping him contact his personal power, "What would you do if you saw a dragon?"

"I'd kill it, open it's belly, give it a present, and tame it. You'll see, you'll even be afraid of it."

Little by little Adrian mastered his fear by talking about everything he would do to the dragon. He was no longer without arms although still not very eager to meet one, not being quite sure whether these creatures belonged to the realm of imagination or not.

After our visit to the cave, and especially after talking about the Disneyland dragon, Adrian was able to go through tunnels without a qualm. He noticed all the tunnels we went through, talked about them but was no longer frightened.

## Fear of spiders, insects, dogs and cats - and other phobias

The most innocuous images can set off a phobia. Not being able to decode them, a small child doesn't always know how to limit their impact and when they follow each other quickly, with loud music, he may feel fear if he's alone.

I remember a woman I had in therapy. She had a spider phobia. She finally remembered having been left alone at the age of four to watch a program about spiders, and had been terrorized by a huge picture of a spider on the screen.

In Western countries, the spiders we bump into are not dangerous. Quite the contrary. They help us limit the number of flies and mosquitoes but maintain their bad reputation. Children are not naturally afraid of insects. They often take them in their hands and feel them tickle. It very much depends on other people's attitudes since fear is very contagious. If an adult is afraid then there must be danger and children reproduce that fear.

Unjustified or disproportionate fears can also be the result of the projection of different sorts of anguish onto objects other than the true cause of fear or anger. For example, a spider will spin its web and paralyze its prey. The frequent spider phobia can be seen as a symbolic projection of the intrusive mother a child is unable to escape from.

In the cellar or the cupboard under the stairs

Just like the fear of spiders, this fear is typical of one transmitted by the parents or other children (older cousins etc.) Nonetheless, the cellar is a strange place. It's not one you pass through as you do other rooms. It's dead-end where you go to get something. It's not a place you stay in, so maybe it's better not to linger... Moreover, it's cold and clammy and rather dark and gloomy where you're closed off from the outside world.

The best way to to avoid fear is to decide to go there yourself. Children quickly notice when adults systematically get out of doing certain chores. So if someone doesn't like going there, then there must be something unpleasant or disturbing! It's a place that smacks of mystery or even danger.

In France, many adults remember awful times when they were locked up in the cellar as children. As a therapist, I've listened to a surprising number of people who have been traumatized by such childhood experiences. It's a form of punishment that seems to have been less frequent in the Anglo-Saxon world.

Geraldine used to be regularly shut up in a basement when her parents lived upstairs on the fifth floor of an apartment complex. Imagine her unspeakable terror during the hours spent down there. She knew it was a waste of time shouting as she couldn't even hear sounds from above. She just had mice for company as well as a few spiders that got tangled in her hair, not to mention the damp!

Jeremy had been left all night long in a cellar at school. The director had put him there after school because he hadn't worked hard enough and then forgotten him and gone home! His parents were worried stiff at not seeing their son come home on time but the school was closed. That was just thirty years ago and the director was not even reprimanded. The youth continued his schooling in the same establishment but was never again sent to the cellar.

Ben was sent down to the cellar (or to a dark cubbyhole in the loft) for next to nothing. He was told to stay at the bottom of the stairs in the dark and had to stay standing up as well. If he didn't obey he was given a few more hours. If the punishment lasted a very long time he was brought a bit of bread to keep him alive. Crying or making any noise would only condemn him to further parental wrath, with the whip on hand.

## He's so shy!

Adults talk about shyness when a child takes those few minutes he needs to enter into contact. In this way they hide their uneasiness when faced with a child who hasn't yet integrated the usual social codes. The hello that doesn't come out immediately throws adults off-balance, and it's the child who is taxed with being shy! It would be a pity to let that label stick to your child, as it could indicate that he's not quite normal and make him really shy. To whoever calls him shy it's easy enough to say,

"No, he just needs a little time to get to know you."

Children need a few moments to take in what's going on and feel safe. It's very nice for adults to see children saying hello without paying attention to who they're saying it to but it's a sign of submission and more reflex obedience than true politeness.

A short period of observation is necessary but varies according to the child. It's a real need and may take twenty minutes before the child feels ready to approach the other person spontaneously.

## What about the fear of school, teachers, marks...?

The best way of finding out what's really happening is to take the time to really listen. What is he truly afraid of?

Could it be your reaction, that of your partner, the teacher or other children?

Tests in school have become over-important and many parents react badly to bad marks. At the very moment when a child in difficulty most needs to be understood and encouraged he may hear the threat of future unemployment. A zero carries a negative career perspective, which doesn't help a child to feel confident the day before a written test.

Lurking behind the fear of bad marks there may be fear of the teacher because of his comments or judgement. Too many teachers are very disparaging and some go to the extent of using humiliation as a teaching method.

Is he afraid of his teacher? Doesn't he want to go to school? Your child needs to be listened to and the situation examined carefully. Systematic support of the teacher is not fair. If your child is afraid it's important to to know how to help him face the problem.

**You are not taking the risk of destabilizing your child if you express disagreement with his teacher.** Even if he has to endure a teacher who's not nice to him for a whole year, **knowing that you find it unjust will help him not to feel low self-esteem but feel confidence in himself.** Knowing you support him will help him put things at a distance and not have his confidence destroyed.

In the USA corporal punishment was forbidden in 31 states in state schools between 1971 and 2011. Bills are still being presented to forbid it in all schools. In the UK, corporal punishment was forbidden in state schools in 1987 and in so-called 'public' (private) schools in 1999. In France corporal or humiliating punishment in schools was forbidden in 1890, although many teachers dealt out slaps and pulled ears even recently.

If his teacher goes too far, whether physically or psychologically, it's important to do something about it and demand that the law be respected. Your child needs help not to harbour feelings of injustice that he's powerless to fight. Such feelings are not conducive to learning or happiness.

Clara, aged twelve, has been insulted and called "fatty" by her teacher. Paul, aged five, has been called a "mongol" because he didn't understand an instruction. Insulting language is far too frequent and absolutely intolerable. Children often don't dare tell their parents. It's not easy to confide in someone when you've been humiliated and are feeling ashamed.

A teacher's over-authoritative behavior, injustice, irony or threats can never be normal. Your child needs someone on his side. No adult, and even less a teacher, has the right to hurt a child, make him feel ridiculous or hit him. According to the circumstances, you can ask him or her to change their attitude and help your child find adequate responses to hurtful remarks. It's always possible to go and see the teacher and ask for a change of attitude, file a complaint, take your child out of the class or even out of the school.

Too many parents don't intervene. They say that it won't last, that it's nearly the end of the school year. If nothing is done or said the child will have the memory of the humiliation and even if he is no longer with the abusive teacher, in his mind he will go on hearing his remarks.

Christopher had very bad marks in math. Three days earlier his teacher had shouted a lot and humiliated him in front of the class. His marks consequently dropped, and he was convinced of being a bad pupil. His mother took the side of the teacher, explaining that the teacher shouted to push him on to get better results. She didn't understand that it was exactly the opposite that was happening.

Three years later he changed teachers but still had terrible results. The hurtful things the teacher had said were still in his mind and sometimes, meeting him in the street, would be haunted by that fear and cross the street with his eyes lowered so as not to see him.

I helped Christopher think about his eacher more realistically. Why was it that he needed to shout at a little boy and humiliate him? He obviously felt bad in himself. To bring things back into perspective I invited Christopher to visualize Mr.Whatsit with a red nose, and clown's pants. After two sessions he recovered his mathematical performance. We'd just needed to get to the bottom of the matter. He wasn't the one who was inferior but his teacher. Freed from the weight of negative beliefs about himself and the sequels to the humiliation experienced he was able to regain his intellectual aptitudes.

There are ways to help your child relax. You may invite him to visualize a brief film sequence to re-establish his feeling of being whole. In his mind, he can perfectly well cut the offending character into small pieces, throw a bucket of water over his head, paint his face different colors, strip him naked or dress him in a pink suit with pea-green polka dots. Anything goes and can free him from the harmful memories.

Relationships with other children can also motivate fears. David was terrified a the idea of having too-good marks. It was important for him not to beat Uzi, who was very susceptible about being top of the class and would take it out on him if his position was threatened.

A child may be intimidated in the playground, afraid of an adult or a child, or failure, or going to dirty toilettes or asking for toilet paper – each case calls for specific treatment. We must listen carefully!

# 3

# Crossing over to the other side of fear

Margot is four and a half. We're at the swimming pool, in the sun. She's dressed in a bathing suit with floats. Six months ago at the seaside she enjoyed splashing around in the water even without being able to touch the bottom. But today, on our third day, she is still clinging to me saying, "I'm frightened, don't let me go!"

*First of all, it's important to accept what she's saying.*

"I can understand you being scared, you haven't swum for a long time."

*Then help the child contact her inner resources.*

"Do you remember last Summer how you liked swimming with your floats. You used to go a long way out where you couldn't touch the bottom and you let go of me!"

*It's best to be careful of the voice you use. Mine is admiring. My intention is to avoid making her feel guilty by suggesting that she's silly not to find things so easy, but to remind her of the event and re-create the pleasure she felt to help her feel ready and able.*

"Sort of."

*She hesitates between wanting to and fearing to. The resource evoked is not enough. So I look further back into her life.*

"Can you remember how you got over your fear one time you were afraid?"

"Oh yes!"

144

"How did you manage to get over your fear that day? Do you remember how proud you were? Can you feel that pride in yourself?"

"Yes."

*Sharing our own fears helps reassure.*

"You know, I'm afraid of something too. I'm scared stiff of going on the big toboggan. Daddy went but not me. I'm just too afraid although I know there's no danger, just like you swimming with floats.

*Giving encouragement and motivation helps get over the fear.*

"Sometimes we're afraid, but we go and do it all the same. We can do things even though we're afraid. We'll help one another. You get past your fear and swim in the big pool with your floats, and I'll get past mine and go down the big toboggan."

"I want to get out!"

*O.K. it's never wise to insist!*

She needs time to decide for herself and not just to please me. Here, this is all the easier because I really am scared of the toboggan and she knows it. She knows that if she goes to swim in the big pool, she will be facing me with something difficult. Fear is negative anticipation, and what we need to do is transform that into positive anticipation. The passage from one to the other is possible only if the child feels perfectly free to choose. She gets undressed and we get dried. A few minutes later, she says, "Mommy, will you put my bathingsuit with the floats back on?"

*It is absolutely necessary that Margot sould be the one choosing to go.* The decision, "I'm going to do it" shows that the turning point has been reached between fear that inhibits and fear that stimulates.

145

I help her to put the suit back on and off she goes to the pool in a very determined way. Bravely, and apparently without difficulty, she goes down the steps into the water and shoves off from the side! She peddles with her hands and feet. She's swimming, and thoroughly enjoying it. After a moment she tells me off, "Mommy, now it's you turn to go down the toboggan. "

"O.K. It's my turn."

After sliding and screaming down the big toboggan I feel proud of myself. I tell her so and she replies,

"I'm happy too, that I went in the big pool. Now I love it. Shall we go back in? "

*Pride fixes the idea of success and confidence. It's important to feel proud of the victory.*

Children are not reassured by the fact that people are never afraid, but on the contrary that each and every one of us – even parents and adults – is sometimes afraid. A child easily thinks he is the only one to be afraid, imagines that his parents, as adults, are spared that emotion, and easily thinks he's not 'normal'. This, of course re-enforces his feeling of insecurity.

## How to accompany emotions

*1. Respecting the emotion*

It's on this condition that your child will trust you. His emotion must always be respected, even if it seems completely irrational to you. If a child is frightened, it's not a question of being either right or wrong. There is a reason (or reasons), even if neither of you yet knows which.

## 2.  Listening

"What is it that's frightening you ?", "What are you most afraid of?" Remember that "I'm afraid of the dog" remains very vague. You may ask, "Is it the barking, or the jumping up and down?", "Is it the open mouth full of sharp teeth?", "Is it the way the dog looks at you?" Maybe he's afraid that the dog may bite, jump up at him or start licking him with his big wet tongue?

Listening doesn't just mean lending an ear, it also means helping the child to express what he is feeling. Starting a question with 'why' is likely to lead you astray as it will incite the child to provide you with an answer that's plausible but not necessarily related to the experience. It's wise to hold in mind the fact that he probably ignores the real reasons for his fear.

By listening, you will help him find them, by reformulating what he says and asking more oblique questions following on from, "What…? How…? Do you…? Are you…? (This sort of questioning will be described below in chapter X, Ideas for living more happily with your children)

## 3.  Accepting and understanding

"I understand that you're frightened. That dog is really very noisy." The child needs his emotion to be acknowledged. It's within his rights to feel what he's feeling and we can approve of him expressing it. It's no use trying to 'cure' him of his fear or resolve the problem for him. All he needs is compassion, empathy and time.

147

We're there to accompany a child trying to master his fear, but only in accordance with his wishes. Any particular expectation from us will only hinder the process

## 4. Dedramatizing

As soon as he has been able to voice his problem, you can speak about your own emotions, whether present or past, when you were a child. Did you have a similar fear, or some other one? Why not share it with him? You don't have to pretend but can tell him the truth, preferably choosing a fear of something else so he can feel stronger than you about that and feel more capable of facing his own fear.

## 5. Finding resources from within and without

We've all had the experience of having gone through and surmounted a fear.

"Do you remember a fear you once had that then disappeared?"

If the child can't spontaneously remember, you can help him: "For instance, the first time you were invited to sleep over at Steven's house." He may need a moment or two to remember and relive what he felt at the time. "And then you decided to go. Do you remember how that happened? And do you remember how it went? You came back home so thrilled. Do you remember how you felt?"

"You see, you've already been afraid of something and then gotten over it. Do you think you can use that experience to help you with feeling less frightened of the dog?"

A few minutes to think it over will allow him to get into the positive feeling.

## 6. Helping him unleash his energy

When we're frightened our diaphragm is contracted. Everything that helps us to relax our diaphragm helps evacuate the fear: deep breathing, singing, shouting, laughing… Invite your child to breathe in deeply until he no longer has that feeling of oppression. Sing or shout with him to help him find his voice. Then he'll feel strong and ready to face whatever situation is worrying him.

If he can't manage that, feeling too shy to start shouting, suggest he might think of someone who wouldn't be afraid in that situation, a friend, a friend's father or mother, the garage mechanic, Hulk, Spiderman, Captain America, Tinker Bell, or yourself! Invite him or her to imagine doing something and then getting into the character. Help your child feel strong, empowered and at ease, and say, "Can you feel all that strength and confidence? I think you can decide that it's yours too!"

## 7. Satisfying the need for information

Your child has found his resources. He will now need a bit more information – like knowing if the dog is dangerous or not.

You need reassurance and information when you're frightened but if it is given too soon, it cannot be heard or integrated. That's why explanations are so often useless. You need first to listen to an expression of the fear in question and accompany the child to find his personal resources. Only then will he be able to pay attention to your explanations. And it's even better if he can find them by himself, "How can you find out if he's dangerous?"

149

He can be helped to think it out. For example, you can go to the local library and borrow books about dogs and give any extra information he won't be able to find himself. He'll be able to use this technique in other circumstances. The more autonomy he has to lead his research the stronger he'll feel when facing his fears.

## 8. *Looking at different ways of dealing with fear*

According to the circumstances, you may stop at just one satisfactory solution or ask your child to name a few. It's not a question of saying whether his ideas are good or bad – they have the merit of existing. He's the only one who can estimate their suitability.

"Why not ask the dog-trainer if you can pet his dog? It's just an idea, what others can you think of?"

The different ideas he suggests can be reviewed and assessed.

"So, if you do that, do you think you won't be so frightened? "

"What could make you want to pet a dog and not feel frightened?"

Instead of FEARING TO it's good to think WANTING TO. What will make him want to stroke a dog, go into the water or down the slide? It's crucial that he should not feel under pressure, that you don't expect your child to get over his fear there and then. Otherwise, he will feel obliged to satisfy your wish. And constraint creates fear!

Only a free choice can give the feeling of controlling what's going on and enable a child to get over whatever fear he's grappling with.

# 4

# Using stage-fright

It's the day before the end-of-the-year show that the school is putting on in the Town Hall. A public of three hundred people is expected. Margot has said nothing but I well know that performing in public is always stressful, especially for a little girl of four who's going on stage for the first time. How can we prepare for this sort of experience?

"Aren't you a bit afraid of dancing in front of all those people, or do you feel good?"

"I'm a bit afraid."

"Well, that's normal. I wanted to talk to you about it because when I give a lecture in front of a lot of people, I'm rather afraid too. My heart beats fast, my tummy feels all tight, my hands are sweaty and my throat's dry. In fact, when you feel all that, it's because your body is getting ready. A lot of things happen to give it the energy to dance, sing or talk. Have you ever felt that inside yourself?"

"My heart beats fast when there's a dog barking."

"These are all things that show you're afraid. Fear makes you fill up with energy to face a danger or prepare for something difficult. In fact, the fear we feel when we prepare ourselves for a performance is called stage-fright. It's perfectly normal. Everybody feels that way in such moments. When you go on stage, you'll feel afraid because your body is getting ready to do the best possible. So, when I feel that, I'm pleased. I know I'm getting ready and I breathe deeply. I feel my feet solidly on the ground and I look at the people. I say to myself that I like them and am pleased to talk to them. I send them rays of light to feel more contact with them. That's my way of doing it. I had that idea to slow down my heart when it beats too fast. You can try different things and find your own idea. Anyway, when I start talking, I use the energy in my body and the stage-fright disappears. Do you know what you can do to feel better?"

"Yes, I've got an idea!" she said happily after thinking it over for a few moments. She said no more but a few days later she was obviously thrilled to be on stage. She enjoyed dancing and really looked at the spectators. Her teacher had to remind her that it was time to leave the stage to let the show go on.

Some fears are useful by announcing danger and preparing the body for action. Others are exaggerated, for we don't have poisonous spiders, road drills are noisy but not dangerous, dogs behind fences can't get at us and when we have floats we can't drown.

**Useful fears are to be obeyed. It's no good taking unnecessary risks. The others can be overcome, as long as we decode ourselves and feel proud afterwards.**

# 5

# Is he easily frightened?

Does he feel almost permanent fear? Is he constantly anxious or inhibited in a lot of situations? Does he panic for next to nothing? Is he getting into a habit of high emotivity and fearfulness? Then it's high time to give him some help.

The root of the particular fear that stifles all other emotions can be of many sorts.

## He's overprotected by his parents

"Don't walk on that!"

"Careful, you might fall!'

When the parent tries to prevent all confrontation with danger then he transmits the messages, "the world is dangerous" and "you can't cope with it".

Let's be coherent! Children often receive contradictory messages. Their parents tell them not to be afraid, but as soon as they start becoming more independent, then they're told paradoxically "Be careful" or "Watch out"! How can they figure it out? On one hand it's "Say hello to the lady" and on the other "Don't talk to strangers".

If a child hesitates to immediately greet someone he doesn't know (and waits to see before he hugs and kisses) he will be accused of shyness and being afraid of people! If a child runs up to everyone he meets his parents will reproachfully lament that he's ready to go off with anyone!

Just think about what a child experiences when faced with what might be called double bind[5] situations when contradictory orders are dealt out.

By trying to avoid all hurt, there's the risk of causing an even greater one, which shatters pride in ourselves and the idea of our capabilities. Playgrounds are very safe nowadays even if it's always possible to get hurt. It's better to teach a child how to run, jump and fall, find his physical possibilities and limits rather than have him sit on a bench where he is likely to stay for life!

He may be bitten or beaten up by a friend or get bruised or sore for a few days. He may fall off the swing or over a low wall. He'll get a bit hurt. So what? There are very few really serious risks. Sometimes, a few bruises will teach far more than well-meant advice on taking care.

Over-protective parents tend to lead to either inhibition or risk-taking. If too much is forbidden a child may be led, paradoxically, to want to explore beyond his limits. If he is suddenly allowed to do something he was formerly forbidden or if he decides to give himself permission, he's likely to be far more reckless than others who've been able to find their limits progressively and feel responsibility towards themselves. Just ceasing to be over-protective can be construed as giving permission to do something.

Ceasing to be over-protective doesn't mean leaving a child alone with a difficulty. It means sorting out the difference between misplaced parental worry and real danger. To really help our children, we must be careful about our attitudes or little phrases making them think they are incapable of doing something. Being over-protective can infer lack of confidence. So, let them feel you have that confidence and know that they can cope with life.

It's by trusting our children that they'll feel trustworthy.

## Repressing anger

His rage may be very intense but either he doesn't allow himself to express or even feel it, or his parents don't. A lot of elder children are shyer than their younger brothers or sisters. They are often the ones that don't dare show their jealousy. They repress their anger against the newcomer who has taken their mother away from them.

A child who can't express his anger is afraid of his own violence and of the other's possible revenge. In order to protect himself from emotions that are too intense and would make him feel guilty he unconsciously refuses to feel his rage and attributes it to something else. He is maybe afraid of others because they carry his violence. So he is wary of people ("they'll hurt me"), of his friends ("they'll laugh at me"), dogs ("they'll bite me") or cats ("they'll scratch me")

## Parents' denial or repression of their own feelings of fear

Children are extremely attentive to what their parents are afraid of. In the street if you jump when you meet someone he doesn't know or if you feel worried about meeting someone, your child will immediately feel it. If he's aware of what's going on he'll ask you, *"What's wrong Mommy?"*

Otherwise he'll just look around looking worried and feeling uncomfortable, without knowing why.

William is three. He's afraid of anything that's new and doesn't go towards people. It was obvious that his parents didn't have many friends. They went out very little, avoided taking William into shops, the metro and shopping malls because they thought they were not good places for him to be. It's quite true that they're not places where children usually have much fun but they're part of daily life in society nowadays and, without dragging children there all the time, it's problematical to keep them away.

In order to relieve a fearful child of a fear that doesn't belong to him, but rather to us, it's a good thing to talk about ourselves and let him know that he mustn't receive our parasitic emotions. Of course, it's much better (and much more comfortable) to be healed of these by our personal introspection by work on ourselves to understand our hidden feelings rather than be an unconscious prey to them.

Yanna came to consult about her daughter Daphne who felt terrorized in the playground. In fact, Yanna was the one who was afraid. She feared that Yanna would suffer what she had suffered at school. Once she had identified the problem, she immediately talked to Daphne about her past fears that she had never been able to cope with. The next day, back from school Daphne happily announced to her mother, "There, I'm giving you back your fears Mommy." From that day on, her transformation was spectacular. Daphne became happy and was no longer worried. It sounds like magic but only goes to show that the right response can liberate a child's natural energy very quickly.

## How to help a fearful child

It's important to understand that judgment is a most unhelpful attitude! He's just a child who has a lot of fears or who doesn't dare show any anger. Could you be the one forbidding anger?

He'll need help to feel his personal power and build up self confidence and you can give it:

By suggesting activities corresponding to his possibilities.

By allowing him to find ways of expressing anger.

By encouraging his creativity.

By finding activities, places, games from which all judgement and assessment are excluded. There are now more and more workshops where a child can explore, produce, express himself **without any form of judgement (whether positive or negative) being passed**. Arno Stern's free expression workshop is an excellent example. Children can paint without being criticized. The child, his feelings, his rhythms and his needs are all totally respected. And he gets a lot of attention.

The contact with big animals is often very helpful. Poneys and dogs don't judge or demand. They trustingly allow children to approach when they're ready and have a reassuring presence.

Computers don't judge either and show themselves to be infinitely patient. Children can do, undo and redo things without the slightest show of annoyance. As long as an adult is not there waiting for a result, children can explore, discover, experiment with the mouse and little by little, gain confidence in their prowess.

By taking stock of your own fears and getting rid of them.

To put it briefly:

A child shouldn't be made to face his fears too directly. Give him the means to face them at his own pace and overcome only what he freely chooses to.

# Chapter V

## Anger Serves the Feeling of Identity

How many parents have felt mortified, whether in the park or the supermarket, with their offspring rolling on the ground screaming while people look on accusingly?

And yet anger is a natural and healthy reaction to frustration.

# 1

## Anger is a healthy reaction

Lily's face becomes tense. She's three and storms:

"It's not fair, *I* want to ride!" She gets red in the face and clenches her fists. She's angry. She refuses to accept the verdict of the ritual *"One potato, two potato, three potato, four"* which designated her sister as the one who could ride the bike. Whatever the means of choosing, she doesn't agree because she wants to ride the bike and feels very frustrated.

The only advantage of that way of choosing is that it isn't done by an adult. It's random and a question of luck, implying no parental preference for one or other daughter. But you can't always expect small children to accept their lot without protesting.

"Please Mommy, I've finished my ice cream. I want another one."

"No, one's enough."

Just imagine a child of three saying: "All right Mommy, I understand that one's enough."

What would your reaction be? Wouldn't you feel rather uneasy that a child should not only not assert but cancel her desire? A child like that is likely to be unable to know what she wants. She'll often wonder what she should do, whether she's right or wrong, but won't have the slightest idea of want she would really like. She'll often leave others to decide about her life and need opinions from Tom, Dick and Harry in order to make decisions. When a child insists,

161

shouts and makes a nuisance of herself, she's asserting what she wants and that's very important. Of course, it's noisy and quite an ordeal for the parents, tired after a day's work or maybe having forgotten their own anger. The response can often be violent, confirming that the child's anger is misplaced and dangerous.

Saying "I want that!" is continuing to assert that *I* exist and that I have rights. If the other person refuses, that's his problem but I know I have the right to *want*. A child doesn't necessarily need her desires to be satisfied.

A fœtus is fed via the umbilical cord and gets automatic satisfaction of her nutritional needs. It is part of her mother and doesn't feel any need in that prenatal situation, as far as present-day theory leads us to believe.

After birth food doesn't come so regularly. A baby cries when she doesn't feel right in her body. She doesn't know what it is, but her mother will name it hunger and satisfy the need. Then she'll feel right again.

If her mother doesn't come she'll cry louder. Her anger is a call, she insists on her need and she wants her mother to come and link up with her again.

Anger is too often seen as a way of pushing the other away. That happens with violence, but anger is quite the opposite. It's the expression of a need and a request to re-establish equilibrium, a state of non-need.


## Building up frustration tolerance

Anger is also the first stage of learning how to separate and renounce. When children get angry because they can't get something, their emotion helps them feel whole again and thus be able to accept the frustration. Certain parents feel exasperated when they've explained to their children that something is absolutely impossible and see them furious. They don't realize that it's a necessary, natural and normal stage of learning about not having.

The stages towards acceptance are:

**Denial**
**Anger**
**Negotiation**
**Sadness**
**Acceptance**

All these are natural and important stages. Acceptance implies anger that has been met and dealt with beforehand.

Giving satisfaction by anticipating a demand could prevent a child from both feeling her needs and experiencing frustration. An over-attentive mother who anticipates the slightest desires of her child (mothers are more often trapped in this behavior than fathers) may make the way her child builds up her identity more difficult. Reasonably-dosed frustration is formative. Fortunately, it's impossible to permanently content a child. It happens that all the shops are closed or there are no ice creams left, or there's only one bike for two, or a favourite plate is broken, or both parents are off to work, or Jimmy is away with his grandparents. A certain dose of frustration is inevitable and also useful on condition that the emotions, particularly anger, are duly heard. Nonetheless, unwarranted, arbitrary or too great frustration can be destructive.

A baby depends on her mother and can't survive without her. If she doesn't come quickly enough (a few minutes!) terror will replace anger, the terror of being abandoned and losing the bond. For a baby, living in the present moment, time doesn't exist and five minutes seem an eternity. She has no way of knowing what's keeping her mother away. After a certain time (variable according to past experiences), if no-one comes she will resign herself, quieten down and withdraw into herself. Her body integrates a message saying, "I'm not allowed", "I'm not important" or even "I'm bad", for there has to be a reason why her mother is not there. She can't consciously deduce anything and the process remains unconscious but, if it is sufficiently repetitive, such belief will mark her for life.

Letting a small child cry is plunging her into a world of terrifying emotions. Need/demand/satisfaction. That's the sequence which must predominate so that the baby is imprinted with the knowledge that you love her, that she's important for you, that she's 'good' – safe and sound. It may happen that her demands cannot be satisfied, but her anger has to be heard and respected.

## Facing injustice

Anger also serves to express the feeling of injustice. It's the reaction to a form of intrusion and a protest against what we don't want to tolerate. Anger goes with identity, allowing us to defend our territory, our body, our ideas, our values and our integrity. It gives us the strength to assert ourselves, to say NO and to feel that we are who we are. Someone who doesn't feel and can't express anger often feels a victim in life and quite powerless. Expressing anger enables us to feel our strength, be respected, avoid being damaged by suffering due to a lack and re-establish harmony in our relations.

Harmony is a Greek goddess and the daughter of Aries and Aphrodite. Aries, or Mars in Roman mythology, is the god of war and conflict. Aphrodite, or Venus, is the goddess of love, beauty and communication. So, that's what we have to remember, this harmony we long for is reached through conflict and dialogue, when the two people express themselves fully not through silence or self-denial.

The child can think, "If you refuse what I'm asking for, I wonder if there's not something broken in our relationship. I get angry to show how important this is for me." Anger seeks to re-establish the contact. We shouldn't break it! Keep the bond and be present, attentive and respectful.

**For most of us there's great confusion between violence and anger.** According to Gestalt theory, violence is destructive, whereas anger is constructive. We lack the vocabulary to clarify the distinction. If the word aggressiveness is etymologically positive (latin: *ad-gressere*, going towards), today it has a definitely negative connotation. I refer to the word anger to describe the manifestation of positive aggressiveness, an expression of our life-force. Anger is showing the person we're facing that we are strong, have limits and refuse to suffer.

Not knowing how to manage our anger is what projects us into violence. Anger speaks of ourselves and of what we need. Violence is quite the opposite as it addresses the other person, with a desire to hurt or destroy. When we feel a need, express it but don't get satisfaction we feel an inner emptiness, as if something was missing. We don't feel right. Violence is the result of an attempt to protect ourselves from the intensity of our feelings by projecting them onto the other person. We accuse the other of being the cause of our unhappiness or distress.

When the accumulation of feelings of powerlessness and fear is too intense, afraid of being destroyed, we switch it onto the other, implying "You're wicked!" Violence is in fact the result of repressed anger and the inability to tolerate such a strong emotional charge in ourselves. Even if it is the expression of a need, it hides more than it reveals and leads to complicated (at the best) or inextricable (at the worst) situations.

Violence is the ultimate attempt to make some message heard but since it's disguised very few people understand it. Who hears the schoolboy's distress when he attacks his teacher? Who understands the despair of an inner-city youth tagging all over the place and doing hold-ups? They are both trying to draw attention to the sort of lives they're living. They're denouncing their everyday lives, saying it's intolerable. Who listens to them?

Projection is a universal reaction, a basic mechanism. Giving the message "You're bad!" signs the difficulty for children to tolerate the unhappy feeling of frustration within. Little by little, by receiving the appropriate attention and the respect for desires and needs (not their systematic satisfaction), they will no longer need to project their anger on someone else. They will know from experience that they can express anger and also stop being angry, that it destroys neither them nor the bond with their parents.

If parents are reluctant to listen to anger, they're enrolling in a power game and competing with their children. They are forgetting that they have a more developed brain, and often react by saying "You're not the one to tell me what to do. I'm not going to be dictated to by a child." As most children don't have the right to express their anger, former rages have remained buried deep down and are ready to burst out. The explosion is terrifying and all the more so because there is huge suffering underlying the anger, that of not being understood, not heard and not loved. Repressing anger in your child is a way of holding down your own childhood anger and refusing your inner child.

Anger is a management tool for frustration. It isn't to be pushed away but experienced and overcome. There is healthy, non-violent anger which is formative and also displaced anger that may be excessive, violent and destructive. The first must be listened to and the latter decoded. All are to be respected as they all correspond to a need.

# 2

# Decoding the underlying need

My son Adrian sprang his biggest fit of anger when he was about a year and a half old and we were in the bookshop at a railway station in Paris. We were off for a few days' holiday. It was 2 o'clock and he had gone to sleep in the taxi. Woken up on our arrival at the station, his too-short nap had been interrupted after half an hour. At the time, he was captivated by all the coming and going around him and didn't express any particular annoyance. With a bit of time in hand, we went to buy some magazines.

In the shop, he immediately spied some chemically-colored candy that I didn't approve of and didn't want to buy. I tried negotiating, suggesting all sorts of things like toy cars, trains and motorbikes and soon, but to no avail. He screamed, shouted, and rolled on the floor, fighting me off. He was 'beside himself' and I'd never seen him like this before. What on earth should I do?

One option was to buy him the candy, but it didn't seem the right solution. On one hand, it wasn't good for him and again, his anger was so intensely overpowering that it couldn't be just a question of candy. If I had given in for that, I would have been short-circuiting his emotional discharge. He was howling for the candy but in fact he was on edge through lack of sleep and intolerant of any frustration whatsoever.

As parents we all know that such crises happen when the child is worn out, as this was the case, and doesn't have the necessary nervous energy to cope with frustration. In this situation Adrian was feeling a vague discomfort (his tiredness) and looked for the first opportunity of expressing that something was wrong. No he didn't want the green car, he wanted the candy or the teddy bear his sister was holding. Or maybe the soup was not to his taste… He had to find a reason to focalize his energy and get rid of it. His neuronal buffer wasn't working and an explosion was inevitable, even necessary, as a child can't keep such an emotion in leash but has to let off steam!

Telling him off would have served no good purpose, as he was incapable of doing anything else. Interpreting the crisis by saying: "Yes, I know you're tired" would be thought a humiliation and could only increase his rage. It was a question of looking at the real need and let him satisfy it, quite simply! So I accompanied Adrian through this tantrum, just by being there close to him and looking on. As soon as I could I took him in my arms so he could feel contained and I spoke to him. I said I was sorry to have chosen such bad timing for his nap and that he was right to feel angry.

His sister had chosen a toy so we bought a toy motorbike that he was incapable of choosing at the time but loved once we were in the train and he had caught up on his sleep. There had never been any question, when his sister opened her present, of saying: "Too bad, no present for you, you should have behaved better" when he hadn't had the *physiological* possibility.

His anger seemed excessive because it had been shifted onto the candy. He yelled until his real need was satisfied five minutes later: sleep.

It's not a question of satisfying a demand just because a child is angry. A child's rage sometimes allows us to measure the extent of what she wants or needs, then we can revise our decision and possibly give her what we refused at first. We mustn't be afraid of appearing inconsistent. If it's not systematic the child will just see that you're paying attention to her needs. Capriciousness is an adult concept. A child rarely initiates a power game with her parents. In therapy, when we decode this sort of game, usually the parents discover the role they have played, involuntarily taking position in the game by mistaken interpretation of the child's demand, thinking it too exacting or even a devious way of obtaining something. It's normal that the child should try to resist and that's when grownups often conclude: "He's testing me, he's driving me mad."

Children do what they can to try to draw our attention to their needs. They don't always know how to put it clearly, nor identify what's happening for them, but fury is a sure sign that something important is going on.

Our role as adults is not to establish limits in an authoritative manner, but to guarantee them. We should be there to use the further-developed intelligence of our brains to identify children's need and help them canalize their energy, restore their feeling of wholeness and repair the ability to defend themselves when faced with injustice.

# 3

# A physiological reaction needing to be accompanied

Anger is a physiological reaction during which increased adrenaline production, dilated blood vessels and an increased level of glucose in the blood vessels in our arms and legs provide optimum muscle function. An angry child is invaded by an immense surge of energy and needs to stamp her feet and throw herself on the floor. When they're little, children's movements are disorganized and they need to feel contained so as not to lose the feeling of their body and sense of being. They need to feel secure in their parent's love and acceptance so as to avoid fear of their own shouting, pain and upsurging emotion. Each and every child needs to receive the message "Your anger isn't dangerous and doesn't hurt me. I'm still here ands still love you. You're still the same little girl or boy."

Later on, as the brain matures, anger still infuses the muscles but the child is better able to find the real causes and put them into words. She knows how to restrict her impulses by mental control, no longer feeling swamped by uncontrollable emotions. She can then intellectualize her feelings, find meaning and formulate what is happening inside.

I uphold the theory that children correctly contained and accompanied when angry will not have irrepressible violent feelings for their future offsprings. Considering that most adults seem to have great difficulty coping with anger in a non-violent manner, we may think that it's high time to treat children's anger in a different way.

Very small children don't yet have the physiological means of organizing their feelings and are easily overwhelmed by tiredness or the accumulation of tensions.

Anna's parents can't understand why she is so 'impossible' after having spent a good day in kindergarten school, happy, interested and concentrated. At home she could cry for nothing and throw a tantrum at the slightest pretext.

During the day she has to comply, listen, stay still and show herself to be a good pupil. All these tensions accumulate without her daring to mention the strain of all this to her parents. So, in the evening she shows them what she isn't in the daytime. She lets go of all her controlling efforts and allows herself release. She's too young to be able to identify, let alone speak, about the cause of her excitability. She is in fact showing that she trusts her parents and can take the risk of showing herself to be angry, something she can't do with her teacher.

PRACTICAL HINTS:

**Listen to the emotion.** You will see how it helps the child if you keep an open attitude to receive the emotion. It's sometimes difficult, especially in public, but hold on to the idea that you're working on your child's future. Anger that is listened to only lasts a few minutes.

**Acknowledge the emotion and link it to the cause,** putting it into words. You may reinforce your acknowledgement with little phrases, according to the circumstances, like "You're right, it's not fair", "I can understand that you're feeling angry, because…", "It's hard to accept that…",

"You're mad because you wanted so much to come with me".

**Contain** the small child. Physical contact is the best way of moving through the anger. In any case, better stay connected. The anger of a two-year old is strong and noisy. She will push you away violently when you try to touch her. Try going away and she'll cry even louder. She may run after you, try to bite or hit you. She's seeking contact. You don't need to do any more than prevent her from hurting you and stay put, just paying attention. As soon as you feel that the worst is over, if you open your arms she'll most likely open hers. If she's not yet used to ending a tantrum like that, you may take her in your arms and restrain hitting. Little by little she'll settle into a cuddle and start to feel secure.

Anger gives a feeling of personal power.

By rolling on the floor, a child shows her powerlessness. If she is allowed to express her feelings, shout and be noisy, then she will able to make contact with this feeling of personal power.

By screaming, a child feels the vibration of rage. It's a very important moment. It's fundamentally important to let her do this without JUDGING, not even in admiration! "Now that's a fine anger" is no better received than "You're not nice when you're angry" or "Stop that row immediately".

Anger doesn't need to be drawn out! Anger that is listened to and respected is very brief. It's no use reactivating the moment when the child's ready to move out of it.

If she's worn out, a loving massage will help her go to sleep much better than isolating her in her bedroom.

For an older child when the fury takes hold of her and sweeps her up, you may invite her to go and shout it out in another room, whether her bedroom, the bathroom or elsewhere. You may stay with her or withdraw, according to her choice. Remember children need connection, it's often a better idea to stay by their side, welcoming the emotional response, helping them let it out. Then she will be able to listen to her anger, feel it inside and express it – even by hitting cushions, without bothering the other members of the family until it's over. This has nothing to do with the order "Go and calm down in your bedroom!" pronounced in an authoritative or exasperated voice. It doesn't mean being sent away, it's expressing respect, knowing that the anger needs space to be experienced. It's most certainly not a punishment but rather a tool that all the family can use. It will help if you model the behavior and go and shout yourself in your bedroom when you're upset. In this case, don't hesitate to say out loud what's happening to you, what you are feeling and how you deal with your feelings, till the end when you announce, "Now, I feel better, I'm calm and I can think about my problem". In some families there's a room devoted to just that, often with a punching-ball or a pile of cushions. A place where you can go and give rein to your emotions, take time, think it over, meditate, get hold of yourself.

Coming out of that room the child is again able to take her place in the family. If her anger concerns a member of the family she will be able to voice a clear demand. If it comes from elsewhere, either excessive or inappropriate, she will have put words to it, come to terms with it and put it in the right place.

When is a child old enough to use this technique? Some children are able to as early as three but a child needs to be able to take a step back from the event, talk easily and organize her thoughts. She can only be ready if she has been prepared to do this and finds it natural. That means having been sufficiently held in comforting arms to later be able to contain herself without them.

If we lack the space we can pummel an anger pillow used uniquely for that purpose, better nobody sits on or uses it. It's the one to be insulted and thrown at the wall. Large movements are better than short and quick movements. Hitting the pillow with fists will not be as efficient as taking it with two hands, raise it above the head and hit. But still, it's better to hit the pillow than hurt your sister.

When there's tension in the family, with all sorts of conflicts between the children, it's a good idea to organize a pillow fight, after having sided away all the breakables! Parents and children can divide themselves into two groups and throw pillows at one another. The difficult energy is released and laughing replaces anger. The fight puts everybody on an even keel and brings the family back together again.

# 4

## When parents get angry

One day, I just exploded and shook Margot and yelled at her. She started crying and then got angry, saying, "You're not allowed to do that Mommy!"

I stopped immediately. She was right, I had no right to shake her like that and frighten her. I was very annoyed but that was no reason to harm her in that way. It's a huge wound to self-esteem to fear your own mother. I listened to my daughter. My fury dropped, I excused myself and took Margot in my arms to reassure her.

Another day, for some other reason, I very brutally said to her, "You're such a nuisance!" She looked at me and again responded with, "You shouldn't say that Mommy."

"It's true, honey, you're quite right." I sat down next to her and added: "I don't have the right to throw 'stone' words at you. I said that because I was so upset. But I should have said '*I'*m exasperated' instead of saying things about *you*. When I say you're a nuisance, I hurt you and that won't help me feel better of calmer. I'm so sorry."

Nobody's perfect and we are so used to projecting our personal difficulties on the other person that it's difficult to imagine that it'll never happen again. But it's so important that the child is allowed to feel and say that it's unfair. Her reasonable anger brought me back to reality, made me aware of what was happening and allowed me to excuse myself. No harm was done. On the other hand, if the child cannot or dare not answer back when an adult (or child) says something hurtful, invalidating or humiliating she can carry that wound for a very long time. If the relationship is respectful all the insults in a moment of exasperation will not automatically do any harm but a single misplaced word pronounced at a sore moment can be a wound for years to come. It's better not to take the risk. Of course, staying in touch with their own feelings rather than projecting them on the child allows parents to be more fully aware of themselves. Surprisingly, attributing faults to children is exceedingly tiring.

## Righteous anger confirms our identity

Some parents are afraid of traumatizing their children and never allow themselves to be angry. They deny their needs and repress their emotions. The problem with this attitude is that children unconsciously take on their parents' unspoken anger and exteriorize it, without being able to know where it comes from because it doesn't belong to them. Children can become real tyrants, enraged at the slightest frustration and, contrary to what we often hear, it's not the fault of the parents' severity or punishments but their repressed anger breaking through into the next generation.

We can and we must learn to say ME. Try it out on your own a few times and see what happens inside you, and then what happens for the children.

Suppose you're angry:

1. *You can feel the anger-energy begin to take hold of you,* so let it surge up and invade your whole body and keep

your mind on the physical sensation without getting side-tracked by ideas.

2. *Then identify the real reason for your anger.*

Your child's behavior set it off but where does it come from? Do you feel powerless? Are you afraid of the way you'll be greeted by the teacher, your child and then your boss if you turn up late at school and then at work? Are you fed up with doing everything at home while your husband takes his time coming back home from the office? Has your mother just called up to complain about her varicose veins? Are you worn out and would like to be able to go and watch your match on television?

*Either* the simple fact of pinpointing the cause is sufficient to calm your anger by redirecting your energy onto yourself. Then you can explain what happened to your child which will teach her to do the same thing.

*Or* the rage keeps a growing stranglehold on you:

If it doesn't concern your child – go to 3.

If it does concern your child – go to 4.

3. *You can tell your children what you're angry about,* giving them the real reason without being afraid of tarnishing the image of your husband, wife, mother, father (in-law), boss or whoever it may concern. It's better to protect the image your children have of themselves by not loading them with something that doesn't concern them.

Why not let them know that you need a few minutes alone to free yourself of your anger and then go away and shout if necessary. Get to grips with your 'anger pillow'. They'll be able to do the same when it's their turn! Visualize the person whose behavior is causing your anger. Shout or shriek at the person as if he or she was there, and if necessary hit the pillow to get rid of the tension.

It's very satisfying, and above all releasing, to shout and loudly express your anger as long as you're fully aware of what you are doing and are not overwhelmed by the uncontrollable upsurge of your emotions.

If you can't go into another room be careful not to shout AT your children.

Warn them:

"I'm furious, it's not your fault, but I need to shout." Then turn your back on them and shout, "I'm fed up." or whatever else expresses your feeling. When you've finished, you can take time to talk about it by inviting comments like,

"How did you feel when I was shouting?"

"Were you afraid?"

"Yes, hearing someone shout out loud can make you feel frightened. But it was nothing to do with you. How come I had to shout like that?"

Expressing anger is a good lesson for them. It's worth taking care to correct any possible erroneous interpretations.

If they say,

"You shouted because I knocked over the glass" look at what's really going on and admit, "No. I got angry at that moment but it was just one thing too many. I was already annoyed because the bank has refused us a loan. A glass is so easily knocked over, it doesn't matter. And it's not your fault if the bank won't lend us any money."

4. *Let's suppose you really are angry with your child and you want her to change her behavior which doesn't respect your needs.*

Don't forget that your attitude is a model, whether consciously or unconsciously. Be particularly careful to explain without accusing. Here's the structure:

*"When you...* (description of the other's behavior)
*I feel...* (my feeling or emotion)
*because I...* (my need)
*and I'm asking you to...* (the precise behavioral request, at that particular moment which enables me to repair the relationship)
*so that...* (motivation for the other)"

Which gives us something like this:

*"When you ask me for pasta, that I cook for you and then you don't eat,*
*I feel angry*
*because I cooked for you and I want it to serve some purpose,*
*and I'm asking you to understand what I feel when I do something you wanted and that you don't eat,*
*so that I can go on wanting to cook things you ask me to."*

*When you leave your pants on the floor,*
*I'm angry*
*because I'm fed up with picking up your clothes, and I'd rather do something else with you instead of looking after your dirty washing,*
*and I'm asking you to hear what I feel, and go and put your pants in the washing basket,*
*so that I can feel happy with you and we can have fun doing something nice together. "*

In spite of it's apparent simplicity, the sentence is complex and demands a lot of self-awareness.

First of all, it's not easy to identify the precise behavior we hope for without going into all sorts of generalization

180

or judgement: "You never listen" or "Sit up properly", or "You're hopeless!" are disparaging comments that come to our lips very quickly.

But of course we are so unused to meeting our emotions that we often can't find the words to adequately describe our feelings. We may get one emotion mixed up with another:

"When you get back at two in the morning, I'm furious at you being late because I'm afraid you've had an accident." That anger is only justified if there's been a specific contract passed between you about the time. Here, worry is the most probable dominant emotion.

Detecting what you feel is difficult and soul-searching, and expressing it is fastidious.

Formulating a reasonable demand straight off, without going into the future promises, is not an easy task.

And finally, it's an art to be able to tune into one's feelings, understand the consequences that frustrating or hurtful behavior can have on the relation, all the while considering the other person and being able to motivate her to satisfy our request. Giving a reason *"so that…"* can sound like emotional blackmail but is in fact the response to the question: "What will change for me, for our relationship, if the other accepts my demand?"

It's important that the other gets some benefit from the deal, otherwise why would she accept to modify her behavior? Nonetheless, the first three phrases are often enough: "When you.. I feel… because I…"

"When you hit your brother, I'm angry because I don't like to think he is hurt. "

"When you come in with your shoes full of mud, I'm angry because it means I'll have to clean the floor!"

The exactitude of the sentence prevents us from going overboard. It confronts us with our limits.

Let's examine what we would feel if we said: "When you refuse to obey, I'm angry because I need to feel stronger than you." Or "Son, when you wear earrings, I'm angry because I'm afraid of what people might say." It's not reasonable to show ourselves to be angry for something other than what concerns us personally and directly. Otherwise it becomes a question of control.

All this demands practice. Don't be annoyed with your children if they say, "You're not nice!" You may decode the underlying message and understand that they're saying, "When you ask me to switch off the television, I'm cross because I want to watch the film."

The best way to teach is always via modeling your responses. Give yourself models for talking about your feelings, handling your emotional responses or the problem you face. Verbalize your emotions, say your thoughts out loud and your children will incorporate this useful behavior into theirs for the rest of their lives.

# 5

# A few hints to avoid violence as soon as you feel like hitting a child

Breathe in deeply to get back into feeling centred and grounded after being literally 'beside yourself' or 'out of your mind'. These common expressions illustrate the fact that in this situation your emotions are not properly contained.

You know you have the right to *want* to hit, but not to actually do it. Emotion is not action.

Listen to what that *want* is telling you: "I want to smash his head in!"

Maybe visualize that on your mental screen.

You can say to the child, "I want to hit you but I won't because I don't want to hurt you. I haven't the right to hit you but I have the right to *want* to.

Listen to your need. Give yourself the means to satisfy it or project that satisfaction into the future.

Focus on the child, seek awareness of what is going on for her and think about her needs – those that have probably caused the behavior in question.

Think of yourself at the same age and become aware of what you could feel at the time.

Remember the love you have for her by looking over happy scenes you've lived together. Her birth for example, your delight at her first steps or the day she gave you a present for Mothers'/Fathers' Day.

Hand over to your partner!

If you're bringing up your child on your own, think about calling up a friend to help ease the pressure you feel.

# 6

## Is he bad-tempered?

David, eight years old, is brought to a consultation by his mother. In class, he's aggressive and answers back to the teacher. Other parents complain because he hits their children.

How do I analyze this? One of his needs is not being met. There is always a positive intention behind a difficult form of behavior. David is trying to say something, maybe about something lacking for him or frustration or injustice. After a short meeting, it would seem that he is bored stiff in class and has average marks of nineteen out of twenty! Why should he accept to spend hours sitting down quietly listening to lessons that are below his level? Nobody listens to *him* so why should he listen to anybody? Nobody bothers about his needs so tensions accumulate and have to find some sort of way out. He might have become depressed or ceased making progress, adopting an autodestructive attitude but his reaction was to become aggressive.

David has a brother three years older who includes him in his games. He's accepted by his brother's friends who take him out to play whether his brother is there or not. He never fights with them. He's a big boy with his brother's friends but in class he feels small. Not only is he bored, but he also has to be with a group of children who drag him back. He hates that.

What has made him mature so quickly? Who encouraged him to be the best in school and be close to his brother?

David hasn't seen his father for years and lacking that presence, his elder brother is a substitute and has become his guide. In fact he is angry with other children for not being his father – and maybe even for having a father. Aggressiveness always hides something that's missing.

His father ended up by calling him on the phone. Although he lived a long way away, David knew he was going to see him during the holidays. The impact was immediate. He became less aggressive, feeling more reassured of his father's love. Unfortunately, many fathers separated from their former family don't often phone and sometimes completely disappear from their children's lives. It's very difficult for these children to avoid self-destruction, via depression and self-depreciation on one hand or projected aggressiveness on the other. They need to be able to talk about the lack they feel, share emotions of anger, fear, sadness or guilt. They need a way of freeing themselves from despair in someone's arms so as to accept the separation and loss.

When aggressiveness seems gratuitous and apparently without object it means that the object must be sought elsewhere.

# 7

# Earthlight on the moon[6]

Phillip and Kate bring their son to consult. Frank is two and, although that's the age of anger, he does seem excessively bad-tempered. His rages occur several times a day and sometimes last for over an hour. His parents can't take it any more and decide they need help.

When I asked the usual questions about their family history, I learnt that Kate's mother had died during her pregnancy. Exploring a bit further, it became obvious that she hadn't finished grieving the loss of her mother. Kate had felt flooded with despair at the time of death. Her mother had left her without even being a real mother to her. Kate had never been able to be angry with her, nor been able to go through the stage of revolt in her mourning. She had repressed her rage and despair.

Like all small children who love their mother and can't stand seeing her suffer Frank took those unspoken emotions onto himself. Children just mop up their parents' emotions and tensions like blotting paper. Not knowing where these emotions come from, they fix them on their immediate environment and get angry for 'nothing'. For nothing? No, it's a way of evacuating the tension of something left unsaid, of some emotion left unacknowledged and thus unassumed by the parents, as in this case.

Kate spoke to her son and clearly explained to him everything she had felt at her mother's death and how he must have felt responsible for her stifled emotions. Most important of all, she said, "You're not here to take charge of my anger or any of my emotions. I'll take care of that. " Frank listened attentively. His irrepressible and interminable fits of anger ceased, to the amazement and relief of all concerned.

Kate decided to go through her mourning process in therapy. She was able to express her rage, frustration and suffering and take a look at her parents' reality. She was able to revise her opinion of herself and feel comforted and complete. Frank was able to express his own anger now that he was free of his mother's.

If a child is particularly bad-tempered, when no lack or injustice seems to be troubling her life, then it could be that she is expressing anger her parents have not dealt with. Such a parent is even more at a loss to understand her child's anger because it is 'borrowed' and because she receives some unconscious benefit from the situation. The child is an unknowing accomplice.

To resume, anger comes in many shapes and sizes, and may seem excessive or gratuitous and may be due to:
- accumulated tensions
- displaced anger
- the expression of an unconscious or unspoken anger belonging to a parent
- another emotion (fear or sadness) being camouflaged by anger, because the expression of the root-emotion is impossible or forbidden: "You're a big girl now", "You can't be afraid of that!", "Only girls cry", etc.

**The response to anger is listening, respect and empathy.**

# Chapter VI
## Joy and Happiness

On Sunday July 11th 1998 at 8.30 in the evening there was an explosion of joy all over France:

"We've won!" The French football team had won the World Cup. If I evoke this past event it's because, for the first time on television, the French were able to see men unconditionally hugging and kissing.

Since that date we regularly see such scenes of overwhelming joy on occasions like the Olympic Games, popular talent-spotting shows and many more where athletes, competitors and participants express their joy unreservedly.

Joy is an emotion that accompanies success and love. It's an expansive emotion that throws people into one another's arms. Maybe that's why we're so wary of it.

The aptitude for joy and happiness is the fundamental wisdom of a knowing heart.

# 1
# Can we learn how to be happy in life?

Roland at the age of forty finds life difficult. He feels depressed, finds it hard to make decisions or even go out. He hardly ever laughs and doesn't know how to enjoy himself. He talks about himself, his father's bad opinion and his mother's over-protective attitude – and also of his brother's death. Patrick was just a year older and died at the age of nineteen. At the time Roland was not able to come to terms with this death. How is it possible to die so young? His life went on without him realizing he had left a part of himself behind. He still hadn't accomplished the process of mourning, something almost impossible, being too great a personal challenge. His parents had treated them like twins as they looked alike and wore the same clothes. From the day of Patrick's death fun and enjoyment were banished from the family environment.

"How can you laugh when your brother isn't with us any more?" Roland quickly understood that all the pleasures in life were forbidden. Many people like Roland need psychotherapy to recover their taste for life as they feel that all joy has deserted them.

What can we do to ensure that a child keeps his natural talent for happiness? The fundamental attitude is not to repress it as Roland's parents did but to live our own life as a pathway to happiness and fulfillment.

When children have to cope with the sadness, frustration and insatisfaction of their parents they are not free to feel and express their own happiness.

I've met far too many twelve-year olds who are not interested in life. Their parents are often absent, worried by their jobs or otherwise feeling a lot of stress. What's the use of living if there's no love or joy around? It's a parental responsibility to be happy, transmit pleasure to their children and not spoil their innate appetite for life. Being happy is a choice. It's not a question of pretending, putting on a show or smiling all day long to hide our difficulties. It's a question of facing reality with our hearts.

How can we put luck on our side to *win* in life? Certainly not by wasting it in order to *earn* a living. That means choosing meaningful work, listening to what our heart advises and where it guides us rather than choosing something apparently sensible that denies our heartfelt reasons. Is it reasonable to stay with someone you don't love any more and then develop cancer to escape from an intolerable situation? Is it reasonable to take on your father's business when you would rather have done something else, and then die of a heart attack at the age of forty-five? Or bear atrocious suffering because you carry the weight of your parents' unresolved problems to spare them facing facts? All repressed feelings, emotional knots and unhealed wounds bar the path to joy. Liberating your emotions, letting distress have its say, letting tears flow, shouting out anger are ways of leaving room for newfound happiness, so deeply rooted is it in human nature. There's the joy of simply feeling alive.

Life is by no means a bed of roses but happiness doesn't come from letting it slip through our fingers. Even though we can feel its presence when we contemplate a beautiful sunset, real joy stems from achievement after effort, togetherness after separation.

## Praise and encouragement

How can we help our children keep their aptitude for joy? By congratulating and encouraging them. Rather than concentrating on what they don't do right, let's watch them and see all the fine things they do!

So, he managed to climb on top of the wardrobe? Great!

He wasn't supposed to? Of course not, because there was an element of danger, but you didn't know he could do that without hurting himself. He showed he could and deserves praise for his prowess.

Whatever he may choose as his domaine of excellence, sport, music, art, handiwork, gardening, mending cars, math, literature or science, you will be pleased to see him accept the challenge and succeed. Prepare that success as of today!

Don't be afraid that he will rest on his laurels. Success usually spurs on to further accomplishments as it serves as encouragement. Failure is what holds us back and fear of failure what spoils our performance.

Help him to feel proud even for small things. What's the difference between someone who'll become an Olympic champion and someone else? It's the fact of having felt the pride and joy accompanying success. The future champion is the one who's had the pleasure of all the small successes. Ask our sports hero who remembers, "When I was little, I jumped two stairs in one go and I thought, 'Great! Now I can try three – super, and now four.'"

And so on. Success fires our motivation to challenge anew. People who haven't had the experience of this feeling and who depreciate their exploits, "Oh it was easy!" don't have the same impetus and perseverance.

## Leaving suffering behind

Learning how to go beyond our limits is always a source of pleasure, whether a physical or intellectual performance. Human beings are curious by nature and the thirst for knowledge, understanding and meaning is strong in us.

But maybe we have been taught that curiosity or inquisitiveness is bad and learnt that learning is boring, laborious, arduous.

All the sociological studies show that we learn better when the task is a pleasure rather than a constraint, better when we're relaxed than forced to keep our nose to the grindstone.

If a child is too happy in school, parents say he's not working seriously. Yet, the best teaching methods involve drama and play. The only drawback with such methods is that for some parents and teachers they seem too much fun and must necessarily be ineffective.

Tests and exams will all happen in good time. The best way to prepare for these is to develop a positive attitude, laugh and stay in touch with our natural resources rather than one of submission and constraint.

It's not by chance that, nowadays, clowns come into children's hospitals. It's an indication that laughter and imagination diminish suffering and enhance healing by bringing joy to the children.

# 2
# Love

If joy is the emotion of success it's also that of love, meeting people and finding one another.

Dare yourself to pronounce 'sweet nothings' to those you're fond of,

"Aren't we happy being together!"

"I'm really happy to be living with you."

"I adore having breakfast all four of us together!"

When I express my joy and happiness in this way, I'm even happier, because it makes the family feel good. I say out loud what I'm thinking inside:

"It's good to be happy." So then we can seize the moment together.

When we are too busy with day-to-day chores or helping with homework, we forget this other daily necessity of 'interpersonal hygiene' as Jacques Salomé puts it. **Emotional 'dust' can accumulate in our hearts and provoke emotional allergies.** How great it is to run with our children, without any particular aim – just to feel alive!

Sometimes, my children's behavior exasperates me. I have work to finish, I'm in a hurry for them to go to sleep and easily annoyed. So, I take a deep breath, look at them and think to myself, "They're only two and four, and they're growing. They'll never be two and four again. I must make the most of it!"

My heart melts. I look at them and love them. The annoyance has disappeared because they're more important for me at that instant than any file waiting to be dealt with. When I'm very old and look back over my past life, I don't want to realize too late that I didn't take the time to see them grow. So, as I watch them growing my heart is filled with the joy I feel at the privilege of living together.

# 3

# Playing, shouting and laughing

"Stop shouting! Can't you be quiet! Stop running around like mad things!"

Adults tend to want to calm down the joyously rowdy behavior of their children. Why? When they have grown up and left home, they'll regret the time when their children were laughing and playing around them.

**Children need to be happy in order to feel freedom to exist and grow.** How can you want to grow up if the world is sad? How can you want to be a grownup that's always serious and doesn't know how to laugh and play?

Invited to a friend's house, I take Margot and Adrian to the children's bedroom and there I am on the floor, playing with a toy plane. There are lots of wonderful toys, including cars with interchangeable parts, Batman and various space monsters quite unknown to me. I explore, manipulate and try out all these wonderful things and really enjoy myself. A six-year old boy is looking at me, amazed. He finds it very difficult to speak easily with me and call me Isabelle. Then he gives up and says, "Why are you playing? You're a grownup and grownups don't play!"

"Well, you see, there are some that do. I like playing. "

"My parents never play."

What a pity! Playing is a way of entering into a child's world, sharing the adventure of imagination, meeting them on their ground:

"I'll be the shopkeeper and you can come and buy something."

Some people say they're too old for that. In fact, it's just that they would feel ill-at-ease, a bit ridiculous or vulnerable. They refuse to be tempted by a step back into childhood. They would have to face their own past, and childhood emotions. If they played they would have to enter a child's world, sit on the floor and be noisy with them. They would be taking the risk of coming face to face with some immense inner suffering which would bring to the surface the distress of what they didn't receive from their own parents. Maybe they weren't even allowed to play, laugh, run and shout. Maybe they so lacked tender loving care that now they can't even cuddle a doll or a fluffy animal.

We have to heal our childhood wounds to be able to play simple children's games, allow ourselves to lose control, feel free to laugh, explore our imagination and roll on the floor.

**Laughing is not just a pleasure it's a healthy physical and emotional reflex**. Laughing frees tension in the diaphragm and is an excellent exercise in relaxation. A good dose of laughter could well help us avoid a lot of crying. Why not organize games of hide-and-seek and pillow fights to be able to laugh together?

A child exists first and foremost through the relation he has with others and **his joy will be one of sharing, of enjoying being together**. Sharing a joke or an encounter are things children love. The disapearance/re-appearance act, as in hide-and-seek, is what makes this sort of game so hilarious.

A small child knows how to laugh *with* but not yet how to laugh *at* someone. The latter involves a distance, and no longer involves shared happiness but a feeling of power, because the intimate experience of joy is absent. When you laugh *with* someone but *at* someone else, that means it's at the expense of the third party. Mockery comes from a sense of inferiority and is revenge being taken on someone else for one's own feeling of humiliation. The power to hurt is used as a means of asserting superiority. Mockery is toxic for the child who uses it as much as for the one subjected to it. When hard 'stone'[7] words are thrown to hurt, they damage both parties. Adults should pay more attention to this form of violence.

Children laugh with you when there's physical contact, a happy relationship, a feeling of complicity, caring and love.

A child can feel purely physical joy (experimenting with his body and its movements, cuddling and tickling, playing with earth, water, sounds, objects), and also more intellectual pleasures like learning, sharing knowledge and asking questions.

Small children are captivated by the discovery of their possibilities. Learning is a source of huge pleasure and pride and it's a joy for everbody to share in this.

# 4

# Accompanying joy

Sharing, smiling, laughing, shouting, kissing and hugging are all active verbs of joy and happiness.

Don't be afraid of noise. Show your enthusiasm noisily. Shout, jump, hug and take hold of your children to share this very physical and expansive emotion. Think about footballers and how they show their joy on victory!

We can also awaken esthetic pleasure in children and participate in their joyous appreciation of the world, "Look Mommy, how beautiful the moon is! Being invited to share a pleasure with a small child is such a privilege."

Name what you see around you. Show and share. You will be gratified with all sorts of delightful questions, like one from Adrian who, right in the middle of his 'why' phase, asked me during a storm when we were looking at the sky ripped open by lightening:

"Mummy, how is it the sun lights up but isn't made of lightening? "

Love and happiness are the basic ingredients of growth. "I love you!" and "I'm happy to be living with you!" are things you can't say too much.

Don't let these be empty words. Say them as much as you like, but always looking your loved one in the eyes or with some other physical contact, and feeling the love and tenderness deep down.

A "Yes, of course I love you!" without taking your eyes off the washing-up doesn't guarantee much joy for the person on the receiving end.

Of course, it's not possible to be happy all the time and it's important not to pretend. However, if you're not happy for about eighty per cent of your waking day then there's something to be changed in your life.

Do emotional knots from far back or not-so far back prevent you from feeling happy? Undo them! It's part of your parental responsibility. Otherwise, your children are liable to burden themselves with your suffering, especially if you never mention it as they are ready to abdicate a great part of their personality in order to comfort a too-sad or too-angry parent.

Look for the source of inner joy. Let's not let ourselves be locked up in depression, routine or severity. It's not really so difficult to be happy and it's even possible in spite of difficult outside circumstances. If we can't manage on our own it's possible to consult and get help.

A parent full of inner joy automatically passes it on to his children and it's the most precious heritage they can ever receive.

Increasing the level of happiness in families and schools means being able to put our children on the road to pleasure and fulfilment.

So little is required. A daisy, a chestnut, a sand castle, a little surprise present, candles for dinner, letting off balloons, blowing bubbles… tender loving care.

# Chapter VII

## Sadness

Four-year old Poppy's face suddenly closes up. She seals her lips, frowns and tears start slipping from beneath her eyelids and then she bursts out sobbing. With her mommy holding her hand, Poppy looks at her cat who's not moving any more. He's very ill. He's dead. She cries hard and long with her mommy, looking at him. Good bye Blackie!

**Sadness is the emotion that accompanies loss.**

It's natural to be sad when you lose your cat. It's an important part of your life, but so is a house, a loved one, a toy a school. **Crying gives us the opportunity of getting rid of the toxins resulting from the pain of loss.**

# 1

## Tears affect us

Adrian, playing in the car with a figurine and fighting over it with his sister, hits it against the car seat and breaks it. He sees it all broken and bursts into tears.

"Shut up, you're making such a ruckus!" yells his sister. I intervene, "It's all right for him to cry", and then turning to Adrian, "Sure you're sad at breaking your figurine. Go ahead and cry." Of course he's upset at breaking the precious little toy that he's so clumsily broken.

But we find it difficult to stand the sight of a child crying, and so we say: "Don't cry!", "It doesn't matter", "I'll buy you another one", "Go on, you'll make other friends", "Don't worry, you're a big girl", "Now, dry your tears and stop crying like a baby" and other such messages.

Our children's tears affect us. For many people tears are synonymous with pain. If a child cries, it's because something's hurting. Does that mean that if she doesn't cry she feels no hurt? It's not a question of just waving a magic wand.

Crying signifies repair work, when something is lost. Tears relieve and heal. It's paradoxical that the people who try to console their children (to stop them crying) are those very same who, after bursting into tears for some problem, will then say: "A good cry does a world of good."

Yes, crying does us good, especially if we can cry in someone's arms, someone who knows how to listen to us and allow the tears to flow. It's good to have a witness who can receive without judging, without advising and without avoiding our eyes.

We weren't given permission to cry when we were the age of our children so we in turn often try to stop them crying.

But to be honest, what do we really want? Is it for them not to suffer or, more likely, not to see them suffer?

"Don't cry!" in fact means "Help me, I don't like seeing you cry, so don't put me in such an uncomfortable situation."

In this case, the children's needs come second when they should come first.

And yet tears are a physiological tool designed to evacuate sadness. Sadness that hasn't been 'cried out' stays blocked in for years.

A child who swallows her tears to please her mother or father will keep the feeling of pain deep down, with an additional dose of solitude. There's no correspondence between her feelings and the behavior required of her. She may seem a big girl but, as an adult she'll be hardened to the extent of not understanding the tears of her children or even of others, and not knowing how to laugh and enjoy herself without a glass of wine to help. It's even more difficult for men.

Tears that are shut in block the path to love. Why would nature give us tears if they didn't serve a purpose?

It's nine o'clock at the poney club and it's time for everybody to choose their mount and their activity. All the children are all sitting down and the head of the club asks them to breathe deeply. There's silence and then she begins to speak: "Something very sad has happened. Pedro, the

Shetland bay is dead. Last night, he fought with the others and got a kick on the head in the wrong place. So he died. "

The children have tears in their eyes, and she continues, "Sometimes there are happy events and sometimes sad ones. Here, we have foals being born and also poneys dying. That's life."

The children continue to cry. Some have already been to see the much-loved poney.

"You have a right to cry. For those of you who wish we'll go and see Pedro in small groups. Those who don't want to ride today and prefer to be with him can stay here this morning. His body will be taken away at twelve."

The children walk respectfully past the poney laid out in the stable, covered with wild flowers that they picked for him. Everybody observes a special moment of remembrance or gives him a last stroke. A lot of eyes are red and tearful. It was a beautiful death ceremony for a poney and a beautiful experience for the young horselovers.

Death is part of life. It's both important and constructive to let a children see or touch a dead animal (only if they so wish), allowing them to feel his pain physically, take the time to say goodbye and fully realize that they'll never see him again.


## What should we say?

Myriam is taking great care in announcing the death of her grandmother to Anthonia who's five years old,
"She's gone and she won't be coming back."
Anthonia looked at her mother and said knowingly,
"Ah, so she's dead then!"

As soon as a child has had the experience of Autumn, she knows that there are dead leaves. She's also seen a fly on its back, withered flowers, a pigeon flattened on the road or has even found her hamster stiff and cold in the morning. Depending on her age, death will not mean quite the same thing. It is said that children only acquire the idea on the non-reversibility of death at the age of nine. That's no reason for talking nonesense.

It's rare to spend the ten first years of your life without meeting up with death concerning someone close to your heart. It may concern a goldfish, a dog, a grandparent, a classmate, a family friend, a brother or sister or even a parent. They don't all have the same importance, of course. What should we say? **The truth and nothing but the truth**.

Telling the truth does not mean brutally confronting a child with a reality she can't assimilate, or using violent images. It's important to take time and respect her ability to understand and assimilate.

If it concerns a grandparent, it also means that it concerns parent of yours, it's something deep you can share. The death of a classmate is very upsetting and the death of a goldfish is sad. A child is in direct contact with your emotions, so it's useless hiding anything. If you do, your child is likely to panic and could equally well stop trusting you. **Something hidden is far more worrying than something explained.** Children confusedly perceive that you're not telling them the truth and then they lose confidence in you or in themselves or both.

If you persist in denial of the truth the child will doubt her own perceptions and build up negative beliefs. This can lead to problems elsewhere. To show you how obedient she is she may also refuse to take in information in class and lose taste for learning.

Psychologists are now certain that the truth is always less harmful than a secret, even if it is painful to hear.

Her father committed suicide. His mother was killed in a car accident? Her sister died of cancer? It's important that children should know. It's easier for everybody to say what happened and then pay attention to the images a child will see in her mind. By listening to what she has to say you will have access to what is going on in her mind and heart. Emotion filters what we hear. Even if you speak very plainly and clearly, she might easily get the meaning wrong.

If you let her talk about the death a few times she can say what he feels or imagines and ask questions, even if they seem weird to you. Listen and correct only when it's necessary to rectify some wrong interpretation or soften something too violent.

It's possible to give a tentative explanation of the reasons behind her father's act, the circumstances of his mother's accident or the causes of her sister's illness. Whatever the reasons, the child feels abandonned by someone she loved and needed. She must be able to express her anger.

Elisabeth Kübler-Ross was a doctor of Swiss origin. Right from the beginning of her work and until her death in January 1999, she listened to tens of thousands of adults and children on the verge of death, guiding them towards that experience and accompanying their families in the mourning process. In her widely read books, she recounts what people confided to her and what she was a witness to.

The stages of mourning are now well-known but she was the first person to map them out. They are very similar when facing the shock of learning about one's own imminent death. Here are the stages through which we human beings pass after the loss of someone dear that children, just like adults, inevitably go through.

The first stage is **denial.** "No, it's not possible. He can't be dead!"

Then comes **anger**. "You're horrid Daddy, you didn't feed the hamster!" "Why did you die and leave me, Mommy. I didn't want you to go away, it's not fair."

It's too early at this stage to try calming children down or reasoning with them, "You know your hamster was old", "I'll buy you another one", "Your Mommy wasn't able to choose. You know she loved you."

A child needs to have the right and the possibility of feeling and expressing anger in order to complete her mourning.

She needs you to listen and accept her distress. You can acknowledge her feelings by saying: "You're really unhappy", "You're angry of course that she's not with you any more. You wanted her to stay with you always."

Then comes **depression**. The child retreats into herself and isn't interested in what's going on around her. She looks into the past and thinks over her relationship with whoever has died. She'll need to cry and talk and be accompanied all the while. Once again, you just listen to and acknowledge her emotions, welcoming the tears without interfering, being conscious that each tear rolling down her cheek is one less imprisoned inside. It's the phase of **nostalgia** necessary before **acceptance**.

After the loss has been accepted a new attachment becomes possible. That indicates that the mourning has been accomplished.

The death of an animal or a person is the opportunity to talk about death in general and all our loved ones. A child's questioning doesn't always imply worry as long as the adult avoids evasive replies. It's the non-answer that's worrying as well as excessive reassurance, "No, I'm not going to die, and nor are you. Only old people die." She's capable of answering back, "The poney died and he wasn't old."

So you have to make things clear and tell the exact truth. Children aren't stupid and well understand that anyone can die in an accident. But if their parents are hedging then they understand that they are afraid and that means there must be some sort of risk. Truth is easier to cope with because the child can then talk freely and ask her questions to find out what she needs to know and gain understanding.

Children talk about death far more easily than we do. Before the age of nine, unless they have to face it via a serious illness, they don't have a very clear idea what it entails. They don't dramatize and are capable of asking their grandma, quite naturally:

"You know, grandma, I'll get your jewels when you die," says Margot at four. A bit later she adds to me, "If she dies, we can send a postcard for her soul. Every day we'll see her by putting a letter on her heart."

Very seriously ill children face death with incredible serenity. They know when they're going to die and talk about it with the most astonishing ease, if only we are able to hear them out without giving vent to our own anguish. When they realize that their family can't hear and understand them, then keep quiet as they're extremely sensitive and ready to sacrifice their need for exchange and reassurance to avoid hurting their parents. Have we the right to oblige them to have so much control when they are the ones in need of comforting?

# 2
# Nostalgia

While Poppy is taking her shower, the dead cat is put in a plastic bag and then a big cardboard box. Her daddy is going to take it to the vet's to be incinerated. She comes down to say a last goodbye to her dear Blackie, and cries her heart out in her mommy's arms. Poppy talks about her cat for several days:

"He used to like being on the sofa. If Blackie was here, he'd be running after that ball. I'm so sad he's dead."

Little by little, the memory of Blackie fades, "He'll always be in my heart. I'll never forget him."

This phase of nostalgia is a natural stage of mourning. After the shock, denial, anger, and revolt against the inacceptable, then comes the sadness.

"Stop thinking about it. It doesn't do you any good", "It's time to move on", "Why do you keep on thinking about all that?" are words we often hear. Sometimes parents buy a hamster or a cat just a week after the death of the one before, but it's too soon for the mourning process to have played itself out and leave the place for a new attachment.

## Knitting yourself back together again

However, letting nostalgia do its work is fundamental. We don't look back on good memories to wallow in sadness but to integrate reality, start the repair work and gradually rebuild wholeness after having lost a part of ourselves.

A child will naturally be attached to the people and objects around her. It can be things like furniture or personal treasures and even the walls of our home are landmarks in our lives. When they're small these things are like extensions of ourselves. Everything around us is part of our identity. All loss means losing a part of oneself.

I lost someone who will never again be part of my life and I look over the moments spent together to take possession of what I gained by that presence in my life, now out of reach. Nostalgia is part of the repair work and I do the tour of the boundaries established with that person, filling in each breach and gap. I dig up hidden feelings, exorcise certain things, include the reality of the loss in myself and then sew up the loose ends.

Such a trip down memory lane cannot be painless and is inevitably accompanied by tears. It's important to cry over each memory to bind it in place, incorporate it as something precious. The other is dead and gone but still leaves a trace in our heart – of course.

## Accepting the inevitable

A baby is feeding at her mother's breast. She feels good, life is beautiful, everything is heavenly. The breast is good. A little later, she's hungry again. Her tummy cries out and she cries out, but her mother doesn't come. The breast becomes something bad, because it's absence is a cause of frustration. The first days of life are marked by the oscillation between a good and a bad breast. This stage is called

214

the schizo-paranoïd phase – *schizo* because the world is divided into two and *paranoïd* because the child is afraid of the intensity of her aggressive feelings.

Then comes the phase of depression. It is not a question of pathological depression but just intense sadness. This stage marks the integration of the good-and-bad object, the good-and-bad breast. My mother is neither all-good nor all-bad. She's sometimes one, sometimes the other, so I give up a world where everything is black or white to embrace reality with it's various shades of black, white and grey. It's sad because I have to give up the ideal mother who is always good and never frustrating. I abandon the idea of heaven, come down to earth and relate to a mother who sometimes gives and sometimes doesn't, because she is a real person with her own desires, who exists outside myself and is not the extension of my desires.

Some people never manage this integration and stay in the duality of black or white and can't see the huge range of intermediary greys.

# 3

# Accompanying sadness

Accompanying sadness just means leaving time for crying. Tears can be encouraged simply by saying "It's hard", "You're so unhappy about so-and-so", "It's sad to think you won't ever see them again."

In general when someone cries avoid body contact unless you're sufficiently intimate and sure your contact will not stop the tears.

You can then take a child in your arms, heart to heart. While you breathe calmly and deeply, feel her breathing and open up your heart. Encourage her to cry it all out:

"You just cry honey, cry as much as you need!"

Tears also help to accept defeat, so avoid saying to Ludmilla, if she hasn't won the game, "Don't cry, next time it'll be you" but rather, "Yes, I understand that it's hard to lose." Does that seem an exaggeration? Try it out. The tears are there anyway and you'll see that they last a lot longer if you don't respect the reason for them.

# Chapter VIII

## Depression

Depression is very different from a momentary fit of the blues, which is natural, normal and inevitable. True depression is a heavy, leaden atmosphere that weighs you down for weeks, months or years.

Depression resembles sadness, but it isn't a healing sadness. It's a knot of blocked emotions.

It indicates an insoluble problem for the child, a profound distress that hasn't been heard.

# 1
## How do we know?

A teenager who sulks from dawn till dusk is easily noticed but in young people depression is often disguised. Depression can hide beneath the surface in a youngster who is excessively docile, conformiste or rebellious and thus go completely unnoticed.

When a child is too good or too brilliant at school very few adults worry. And yet that's one of the signs of depression. A child is a living, moving creature and, if he is too subdued, he's repressing part of of his life force.

Bruno is eleven. He's very quiet and does well in school. But nothing really interests him and he doesn't have any projects or interests. He doesn't know where he wants to go on holiday nor next weekend. Other than the refuge of his computer he has few interests. He's unemotional, rather dreamy and his life slips quietly by. He doesn't take it in hand. It's as if his life doesn't really belong to him.

Let's go behind the scenes. Bruno's parents often quarrel. His father is unfaithful to his wife and both parents think Bruno doesn't know. They're both very careful that he shouldn't overhear a conversation on the subject. However, as soon as he is alone with me it's obvious that he somehow knows there's another woman in his father's life and that his mother is unhappy about it. He can't talk about it with them and never mentions the distress their persistant squabbles cause him. He closes everything up inside. Since his parents don't talk about this with him he's not supposed to know and even less refer to the situation. Moreover, he's afraid of them separating if ever he brings up the subject and no child wants to feel he could be the cause of his parents' separation. He would so like to see them love one another.

When his parents are able to talk about this he will be able to say what he feels, thinks and fears. He will be able to cry and free his pent-up emotions. A depressed child is one who suffers within, a frustrated child, who has no possibility of expressing what's wrong. This impossibility is what sows the seeds of depression.

Another mask of depression, unsuspected by most parents, is agitation. Hyperactivity can be a struggle against depression, and hide an underlying problem. When parents scold, punish and accuse the child he becomes more and more closed in on his distress. Some parents tend to administer Valium or Ritaline rather than look at reality, their child is unhappy, and maybe it concerns them and the way they live[8] or something he's having trouble with at school or outside the home.

If nobody bothers with such a child, the rebelliousness may turn into violence. That's why Martin comes to see me with his mother. He's just hit a classmate in the kindergarten and the headmistress nearly refused to accept him in school. At the age of four, adults and children alike consider him a monster and label him such. In the park, mothers take their children away, he's never invited to play with friends and they don't come to his house. He comes to think and even his mother is beginning to think that he's a monster. Could it be genetic? What can be done about it?

I ask his mother to tell me all about him, from conception onwards. I learn, (as does Martin who's listening) that his father left long before his birth, as soon as he knew of the pregnancy in fact. He didn't want to be a father. Let's put ourselves in Martin's shoes? How can he understand that his father left? Until he has heard why his father deserted home he can only deduce that it's because he himself is inacceptable, a monster. To excuse his father and spare him taking responsibility for his abandon Martin is ready to assume that responsibility himself – he must be the guilty one, he's a monster. From then on, it's just a belief to be confirmed and so he behaves like a monster. Strange as it may seem, children tend to feel more emotional security by taking some blame than by accusing a parent.

One session was enough to transform Martin's behavior. He was so changed that his mother didn't recognize him. Just one session was sufficient to enable him to understand where the maiming belief came from and during which he was told that he had no responsibility for his father's behavior. He didn't leave because his baby was a monster but because he had problems and felt incapable of bringing up a child. Martin has stopped being systematically against everything. Even his bath, that had previously been an ordeal, became great fun. He was no longer violent except one day after school. His mother asked what had happened during the day and learnt that the teacher had obliged Martin to make a present for Fathers' Day!

When a child doesn't feel loved, he tries to find a reason. He can't involve his parents as, for a child, they are always above suspicion and so he prefers to accuse himself. If his parents hit him it's not because they're violent, it's because **he** is the bad one. What is more, most parents transmit the idea: "I'm hitting you because you've done something wrong". It has become a question of 'correcting' the child, not what's wrong. If we examine the situation critically, it's difficult to see how a slap can cure a fault. If the child is *corrected* that means that he is the *fault*. It's easy for him to deduce: "If my parents hit me, it's because I'm bad" Self-depreciation seems preferable to any questionning of the parents' 'right' to punish. A child thinks to himself: "I need them, so how can I imagine that they're vulnerable and incapable of controlling their anger but capable of hurting me. It's easier for me to think that I'm the one in the wrong, that I'm the monster."

## The symptoms of childhood depression

We can start looking into this delicate question when the child:
- doesn't laugh
- isn't interested in anything, saying: "I don't know what to do!"
- is bored
- is an almost too-good child
- is turbulent
- has sleeping or eating problems
- has difficult behavior
- needs adrenaline-producing stimulation (fighting, sodas, sugar, violent films and video games…)
- has learning problems at school
- shows no interest in school work or is too brilliant in class (beware of persistent too-good marks)
- often complains of feeling tired
- is repeatedly ill

- is over-obedient

# 2

# Poor school results – an indicator

Poor school results are very difficult to assume for a child, even if he seems not to care (maybe even more so). It's no use piling it on by making him feel guilty, insulting or humiliating him.

What are the causes? Your child is not stupid, incapable, retarded or anything like that. Something is preventing him from learning at the moment and that needs to be looked into. We need to use our little grey cells to find out what is hindering his learning abilities. We are the ones with an adult brain. Let's explore. Is there another child bullying him? Is there a teacher who's unfair, cold, severe or incompetent? Is there some unspoken problem in the family? Is he in conflict with his brother or mother or with some unconscious expectations of his father? Once again, careful listening is your best tool.

Concerning problems in school, he needs you to be on his side when meeting his teachers. His whole life is at stake. It's terrible to be considered a zero, whatever your age. It's difficult to get back on course after such cruelty. And it's fundamental to explain to your child that he's not stupid and that if he can't do his lessons there's a good reason for that because:

With a whole load of worries on his mind, there's no room for learning.

His teacher hasn't found the right teaching methods for him. Be careful not to invoke too many psychological reasons because he has dyslexia or is maybe more visual than his teacher.

He's bored.

Before he can be interested in his schooling, he must
Feel the school (the teacher) is interested in him and
Feel responsible for himself and his choices.

Whatever the situation, the child has emotions he couldn't find a way to express. Those repressed emotions alter his learning abilities. Listening to him – helping him to voice his worrisome thoughts and sort out these deep emotions will free his capabilities and motivation.

# 3

# Is he often depressed?

- Here are a few avenues to explore:
- Is the presence of one or other parent lacking at home? When you're there, are you available to spend quality time with him (other than that spent on homework, which doesn't count in the shared-time register as you're there for yourself, not for him)?
- Are you, as parents, close to one another? Do you love and respect one another? Whether living separately or together, it's the emotional distance that's most painful for children.
- Are there family secrets that you haven't told him about?
- Does one or other parent suffer fom depression (consciously or not)?
- Is he a victim of, or witness to, violence concerning a sister, brother or parent?
- Has he suffered some sexual abuse?
- Has there been some other traumatic event in his life?
- Is his teacher physically or psychologically violent, unpleasant, authoritative or indifferent?
- Is he bullied at school?

## How can you help?

You can tell him that you can see that he's not happy and that you want to help him. The child will often deny that, saying, "No, I'm fine." If you maintain your standpoint and go a bit further by saying, "When I see you get mad with your friends all the time, I can see you're not happy. Is something worrying you that's not easy to talk about? Maybe you're afraid of how we might take it, or maybe you don't quite know how to talk about it. But I can't leave you like that. It's important for me that feel free to tell me what's wrong."

"I don't know. I get mad at everything."

"What could be bothering you at the moment? Do you have any idea?"

"It's the math teacher. I'm no good at math. I always have bad marks."

You can go on asking 'what' or 'how' questions: "How do you feel when you can't manage?" "What do you say to yourself?" and so on.

Why not give him permission to express himself and be ready to understand without commenting, without feeling guilty, without being upset?

Just listening and going on asking that sort of question will help the problem come to light, so you and your child will be able to sort it out later. It's important that emotions should be expressed without necessarily resolving the problem. No use harassing him for hours on end. As soon as he's had enough, even after a few minutes' talk, you can quit, letting him know that you'll talk about it again, leaving him time to think it through. On your side, you can think it over too. You know your child, his environment and the general circumstances. Where do you think it all comes from?

Playing games and doing activities together will make you more truly present.

Being witness to injustice, invasion of his territory or personal insults can afford opportunities to help him to be healthily angry:

"Okay Max. You can tell your brother that you don't want him to take your bike."

"You may answer back when he says you're a weakling. How can you answer back?"

**De-pression. It's the very opposite of ex-pression.** Vital energy is closed up inside. Anger, the expression of frustration or hurt, is held back. **The more the anger is ex-pressed the more the de-pression is lifted.**

In this way you can help your child build up a feeling of personal power and control over his own life. Accepting his anger with pleasure will give him a sense of legitimacy. Listening to his opinions about everything, whether it concerns the family, school, holidays and taking note of what he says before you make your decisions will help him feel connected.

If he doesn't yet choose his own clothes then it's time he did. If you refrain from commenting on what he actually wears, why not start letting him know what you like or don't like?

It would be a pity to lose any opportunity to show him that he is what is most important for you, so important that you really want to spend time with him. He needs time with you. "I've no time for him", is a very revealing expression to indicate that you don't care for the person in question.

As far as possible, come to grips with your own problems as an adult. If you can't do any more, at least you can talk to him about them and not leave him to carry them on his own, more or less unknowingly. It'll be constructive to tell him that your problems are not his and that you, as an adult must and will deal with them, on your own or with the other(s) involved. It's constructive if you give him the opportunity to disclose his feelings, so you can take heed of his emotions, his thoughts and his needs.

# Chapter IX

## Life is not a Bed of Roses

Failure, pain, illness and death are events in every human life. How can all our ordeals be used constructively? How can we help our children surmount the inevitable sufferings of childhood, mourning, separation, illness…and how can we help them become fully adult and capable of facing the difficulties of life with a wise heart?

# 1

## Do we have to harden ourselves to face the problems in life?

They say that children brought up in a 'cocoon' are fragile and if raised with such cosseting will more than likely find it difficult to face life. I remember the first children to be sheltered in a sterile bubble in hospital in order to protect them from germs they were not immunologically equipped to fight. A baby boy had lived in one from birth and was only able to leave it after several years. He was terrorized by the slightest event and absolutely unprepared for life. However, the bubble has little to do with normal childhood at home. When people talk about a cocoon, they mean a too-easy childhood. How does being born under the best conditions, into a happy family without material problems, with attentive parents who give lots of love and freedom, make children fragile?

Are they so easily injured by life? That's what some people say to justify their harsh way of bringing up children, of teaching them what life's about – meaning hardship. We can translate that by injustice, punishment and suffering. Is that really what we want our children to think life's about? When my daughter was in kindergarten, her teacher told me how important it was that she should be prepared to follow strict rules and regulations because she would come up against them all her life. She was only three!

Children who don't have to submit to excessive orders, who are not hit, forced or hurt are certainly not very hardened, having had no opportunity of building a protective shell but they have developed ressourcefulness. If they get into difficulty their first reaction won't be to freeze but, being sufficiently sensitive and able to think by themselves instead of obeying others, they'll be able to respond more adequately to the situation. Maybe they'll react more than others and cry more but isn't that the sign of a healthy mind? They're more sensitive for sure and that's a very good thing! We deplore the lack of sensitivity in the world in general. How can we want our children to conform to it?

Fortunately, it's now obsolete to interpret the expression of emotion as weakness and inability to assume life, because it's quite the opposite. If hiding one's feelings is useful in power games where the aim is to manipulate and win the battle in the long run it's their repression that enfeebles people, not their expression as long as the latter is neither irrelevant nor disproportionate. The outbursts of rage that darken our brains, tears that sweep us away, fear that paralyzes us, are not emotions to be encouraged, as we have observed throughout this book. They play the parasite on true feelings and, although meaningful, are rarely connected to what's going on here and now. They are to be decoded but their unbridled expression makes the problem worse.

When I touched on this subject during a conference, a young woman spoke up to say that in most companies, feelings usually weren't listened to. She gave a recent experience as an example. Confronted with an injustice, her distress took the form of tears when faced with her boss and he used it against her, saying that she was over-reacting and not able to hold her own. This shows how we convince ourselves that our emotions are not acceptable. She thought she had expressed her indignation. In fact, she had expressed a parasitic feeling, sadness, instead of anger. Anger is the only acceptable emotion when there's an injustice. Tears from a victim are an invitation to a power game, and the boss responded to that.

Our parasitic emotional responses can't be understood by others who feel insecure when faced with feelings that seem irrelevant to the situation. Their response is in consequence and necessarily at odds with our feelings. Only our *real* emotions can be understood by others.

We need to master our emotional grammar much better. Expressing emotion doesn't mean losing grip on ourselves, crying without restraint or for no valid reason other than a sad story in our past. In this situation, it was the case of the former little girl trying to face up to her daddy transposed onto the present-day relationship! Well-placed emotions make us powerful. Inappropriate emotional responses make us vulnerable.

For most people, crying is associated with pain – if someone sobs, it's because they don't feel good. We seem to think we can do away with the pain by doing away with the tears, like some sort of disappearing trick, as if not crying means not feeling. Of course, it's most upsetting to hear someone suffering and crying. But isn't it unfair to expect someone, especially a child, to stop crying and cope all alone because we can't handle their tears?

A child who ex-presses herself is putting her emotions outside instead of keeping them inside. She's unhappy but that doesn't give her emotions the power to destroy her because tears are a means of getting over the pain.

A child who is made to stop crying has to store up her pain in solitude. Part of her psychic energy is used to find meaning for the pain, contain her emotions and try to suffer less. It's energy that's no longer available for embracing life, learning, studying or having fun with her friends. She's likely to be weakened by the strain of it all. Sooner or later, she'll express her distress via a symptom that her parents will most probably not recognize as such. Eczema, bed-wetting, refusal to eat, bad marks, violence or depression are just some of the possible symptoms.

These emotions can stay buried for years, only coming out in the adult. Altering the perception of reality, they can cause professional failure, unhappy mariage, mistakes and conflicts. Such emotions may ex-plose in the case of losing one's job or divorcing, or im-plose with cancer or a heart attack.

Life is strewn with ordeals and there's no need to provoke them just to be able to support them! On the contrary, helping a child to stay on her feet in adversity and get over it without harm is helping her build confidence in herself, in those around her and in her ability to get over her disturbed and disturbing emotions.

The denial of emotions by arming ourselves against them is not only an illusory way of avoiding the problem but, as we now know, how toxic such emotional repression can be for physical and mental health. Emotions are Nature's way of giving us a tool-kit to face the difficulties in life, so why not use them?

Let's review the most common childhood ordeals, but without mentioning any form of cruelty or abuse which are outside the scope of this overview and to which another book will be dedicated.

# 2

# Separation

For a small child, separation is one of the main issues.

## Separation at birth

It sometimes happens that a mother-baby separation at birth is inevitable. Health problems may impose specific treatment and technology unavailable in your hospital. More and more hospitals favor the mother-child bond but it's not always technically possible to maintain. Nonetheless, if you're told "it's impossible", insist and check. Although you're in a maternity ward as a patient, that doesn't mean you have to submit to anything and everything.

My first child was born by cesarian section. As soon as I could go down to my room, I learnt that I would see my daughter an hour later and not before. Since she was small and had a low temperature she *had to* stay in an incubator. She was my first baby and I wasn't ready to resist medical absolutism. Faced with the categorical, "As long as her body temperature is low, she must be kept warm." We weren't prepared to resist, and yet our bodies were logically the same temperature as the incubator. So, why wasn't it possible to take the incubator downstairs to my room?

"Incubators can't leave the ward. And the nurses who prepare those in your ward only start their shift in an hour."

We couldn't believe it! Jean-Bernard picked up the incubator of his brand-new daughter, pursued by nurses who shouted after him, "You're not allowed to do that!"

"I'm taking it. You have no right to leave this baby alone when her mother is downstairs!"

He carried out his project and of course there was no problem.

Nathaniel was another child born by cesarian section, with a delicate heart condition. He was transferred in emergency to another hospital. Because of her operation his mother wasn't allowed to accompany him but his father was able to. He spoke to his baby and held him in his arms. When the staff asked him to leave for the night he quite simply refused. There was no question of leaving a new-born baby all alone and sick in a strange universe. He was going to sleep next to him and he did – on the floor under the cradle! The staff did everything they could to persuade him not to but he was so determined that they capitulated. The next evening he was given a mattress! It just goes to show!

Things are beginning to change at last. Now that parents are showing that sort of tenacity, hospitals are beginning to offer accommodation for members of the family who need to be on the spot.

If the separation is really inevitable, it's a good idea to talk about it. Yes, to the baby. She'll hear, and without understanding the actual words, tune into the intention and your calm acceptance. It's absolutely amazing to see a baby calm down or stop her food strike just because she's been told what's going on.

A baby is a whole lot more than a digestive system, although it has had to be scientifically proved, so deaf and blind have we been to the fact of a baby being person and deserving all due respect.

If she doesn't speak with words, she speaks with her body and cries, trying to communicate and should receive meaningful responses. She needs information and her brain is capable of registering all she hears.

## Time to go the daycare center – a daily separation

Later, when it's time for a mother to go back to work it's also time for the baby or child to go to the daycare center or somewhere equivalent. Since Françoise Dolto's pioneer work, the care of small children has been revolutionized. Practically everywhere the staff are attentive to children's needs. Periods of preparation and adaptation are now usual when parents are welcomed until their child feels sufficiently at ease. Practically everywhere, parents are told they should explain things to their children and that it's important that their children hear about them when absent. A child is not a packet to be dumped and then picked up later, and it would seem right that she may have her say in the matter. She stays in daycare so you can go back to work, having no choice but a right to express an opinion and an emotion. If, after the first few times, she still goes on crying after you leave she obviously has something to tell you. Beware of thinking that it will just pass over. Her cries indicate distress. It's tempting to treat her tears as a refusal to go to daycare or the nanny while you go to work. It's better not jump to hasty conclusions that risk burying a crucial problem. Think it over, imagine what she's going through and try to identify her needs. Does the problem concern someone or the place or some other child? Could it be a reaction to your own anguish at leaving her? Are you feeling abandonned in your life? It's useful to dig down to the real problem so that you can address it.

Instead of feeling guilty, why not talk to her, without telling any lies. You like your work and you're happy to go back to it. Why shouldn't you be? It doesn't take away any of the love you have for her. Tell her about your job. A child likes to see and feel her mother happy. By putting the blame for the separation on some outside factor (your boss, present-day society…) we would be avoiding our responsibility and the necessity of facing a child's emotions. She won't accept the separation any better if you present your work as some outside constraint – on the contrary! Assuming responsibility is more gratifying in the long run and healthier for the child.

It's the same when she has to go to school and maybe doesn't want to. Be careful not to clamp down on her with, "At your age, all children have to go to school." It's not true! School is not compulsory in France, Britain or the United States. Education becomes obligatory (from between 5 and 8 according to the country) but not school. We could well opt for homeschooling. It's *our* choice, for whatever reason, and is not a question of law. How can we be surprised when our children lie and get out of their responsibilities if we are not able to assume ours?


## Prepare by explaining and describing the separation

Even if it's true that babies don't have the notion of time, it's still important to let them know some time in advance about what is about to happen. Even a toddler needs time to get ready. If you intend to go out for an hour in the

240

afternoon, it's enough to let her know in the morning but not just two minutes beforehand. On the other hand, if you intend to go away for a week, it's wise to let your child know at least a month before and more than just once.

In fact, why not let her know as soon as you have decided to go? A separation concerns two people and early communication provides the time to listen to the emotions, to anticipate and bridge the gap between leaving and coming back and invent strategies to maintain the bond. It could be a T-shirt with your smell, an object of yours that she knows well or a photo. By talking it over together and finding the right thing, you will feel close, and then when you're gone, touching or smelling it, the child can relive those moments.

If she's the one leaving, her comforter or something with your smell will help as well as photos, a teddy bear, a special home-made bracelet or whatever makes her feel a link with home and family, reassuring her that they continue to be there in the home even without her.

With an older child you can make a calender for the days you'll be away that she can check off as time goes by. It could be with a little surprise, candy or message each day.

Remember that it's not enough to just mention it once. It needs to be talked about regularly despite reluctance on her part. Her emotions will evolve as time goes by.

• She needs to hear about whoever will be looking after her.

Some children take time to trust someone. An hour-long meeting is not enough and if it so happens that you have to leave your child with someone who's not familiar, be sure they have opportunity of getting to know one another

241

well beforehand. Please don't ever confide your child to someone she doesn't know.

- **She'll be happy to know what she'll be doing while you're gone, so that she has her 'landmarks'** and can feel that she won't disappear with the disappearance of her mother but that her existence continues during the separation.
- **Describe whatever you will be doing, giving the real reasons for the separation** rather than lying or excusing your absence by invoking a outside constraint when it's your choice.
- Let her know what you feel: *I'm sad at leaving you and I'll miss you a lot.*
- Her emotions need to be listened to. She has a right to show anger, sadness or fear.
- It's good to tell her how and when you'll be together again.

## Learning how to separate
- **Play at hide-and-seek.**

Freud described the game of *fort-da*, in which the child throws a cotton-reel attached to a string, saying *fort* (German for 'far') and then brings it in saying *da* (here it is). In this way, playing *fort-da* materializes the 'gone-away-and-come-back' nature of events, just as hide-and-seek will later help the child to cope with absence by associating it with the idea of return. A child only likes playing hide-and-seek in a certain way, needing to choose a place where she will be found quickly, and will go there over and over again. In the same way, she'll cry if your hiding-place is too difficult for you to be found quickly.

- Read stories telling about the departure of a parent, the worries if the child and the relief of return. Then you can talk about the story, "You were afraid yesterday like the baby owls. And then I came back. Mommies always come back. Next week I'm going to be away for two days. Maybe you'll feel alone like the baby owls. There'll be two nights when I won't be able to kiss you goodnight. Then I'll be back."
- **Get her used to the idea gradually.**

As far as possible, plan the separations according to the ability of the child to cope with the absence. For a child of less than two, it's better to avoid going away for more than a day or two, or if a few days, leave her with a strong attachment figure. After the age of two she will be able to say what she feels and wants and you can listen to her.

When should you send her on holiday for the first time? I would think that's it's when she's old enough to express her wishes. It's a good idea to start with a night at grandma's or at a little friend's house and then increase the duration according to how much she enjoys the time away.

- **NEVER go without saying goodbye.**

You'll avoid her tears but they won't be avoided and the betrayal will tarnish your relationship. Teach her to accept and share her tears which are a sign of coping with the separation.

## Contact during the separation

Two weeks seem short for an adult but an eternity for a two-year old.

- **Telephone, write or email!**

She'll like to connect and know you're there and thinking about her. You'd rather not phone so she won't cry? Then avoid calling at a delicate time like bedtime, but do call. If she cries when she hangs up, well that allows her to exteriorize her sadness. Be sure that the person with her will accompany her and won't ask her to be a big girl and swallow her tears.

If she's too busy playing, she knows at least that you wanted to talk to her and that you haven't forgotten her. If you don't call, she could wonder about it without telling anyone. The person taking care of her will say that everything went fine and that she didn't even ask for you or cry. Perhaps she understood that she was not to show any sign of distress. Better be careful, feelings of abandonment can stay buried till adulthood. If your child doesn't show distress, it's possible to re-enact the separation with teddy bears or figurines so that she can allow her emotions to come to the surface and be shared. Once you've set up the situation, just let her play it out. She may need to play that game several times.

Just imagine the absence of your lover for two or three months. It's a time-span that corresponds to a week's absence for a child. The distance is unbearable, you want to take them in your arms and when you speak together on the phone you find it difficult to hang up, fighting back your tears. Now imagine that, being afraid of your tears, there is no phone call, no sign of caring, during all that time. How would you feel about that?

Your child has a right to the same consideration and the same respect for her needs as you do, and all the more so because she's small and cannot satisfy them on her own.

- If you are the parent looking after your child, then listen to her talk about the one away.

"Where's Daddy? " asks Margot (two and a half) twenty times, non-stop. Each time, I answer, "At the office, honey." After a while, I realize that I'm responding like a robot, so I ask her, "And where do you think Daddy is?"

"In his office, working on his computor or maybe with a client."

In fact, she was not seeking a reply to her question but giving herself a mental image of her father to feel closer to him.

"You're thinking very hard about your Daddy", would have been a better, more understanding reply.

Sometimes the people around prefer not to talk about the absent person to avoid any undesirable emotion. Too great avoidance can seem strange to the child and worry her. It's better if she can speak freely and say what she feels and thinks.

## Together again!

- **Don't be surprised if your child doesn't greet you immediately or with pleasure.** She'll need time to take in what's happening.

She might need a few minutes to realize the good news, that mommy or daddy is back. She may need to finish what she's doing but don't think for one minute that it's because she's not interested in your return. On the contrary, she wants to feel whole before going to greet you, so she may take a little time to put away her marbles or finish drawing.

- **Be careful not to throw yourself on her and cover her with kisses.**

245

It could create a moment of insecurity. Yes, even kisses can be worrying if they come too hot and fast! It's better to open your arms, squat down to her level and let her come to you. Being the one who decides will help her recover from feeling helpless about your departure.

- **Sweet as sugar at nursery school but infernal at home.**

She accumulates tensions all day long that she doesn't let himself show in front of strangers. She keeps them for you because she knows you will be able to accept them and contain her in that state. You'll go on loving her even if she's grumpy.

- **Your child makes a face when you come to get her.**

Maybe it suits you, because you need a bit of time to yourself and think a bit too quickly: "She doesn't want to be with me" and then go and do something else. You've just missed out on a good time together. Your child is angry because you weren't there. She's missed you and that's her way of saying so. She needs you to spend time with her, to reconnect. In order to repair the absence, she wants to check that you still love her, feel interested in her and want to play with her. What a pity to disapoint her!

Rather than saying: "When you've finished sulking, you can come and play!" you can say straight off, "I understand you didn't like me being away. I missed you too. Now let's play together."


## The first emotional ruptures

As mother and father you, the parents, are the foundation of her existence. Then comes the rest of the family and the whole assembly of grandparents, aunts and uncles. Parents tend to ignore the importance of these close relations.

If a child is looked after by a nanny or someone at home or elsewhere, there may be a change due to retirement for a nanny, studies for a baby-sitter or return to her home country for an *au pair* girl. Let your child know as soon as you do. Why not take photos to keep happy memories alive. Think of asking the person to talk with the child, explaining the reasons for the change and, as far as possible, allowing time for prolonged goodbyes.

There are so many reasons that result in the friends from the first years in school no longer being around. Our society has become so mobile, and people move all over the place. If your child doesn't mention such disappearances, it's more likely that she doesn't know how to rather than because she doesn't feel anything.


## Moving

A move is always the occasion of some rupture in relationships and will be better stood if the child feels self-confident. If she has little confidence in herself, losing her bearings can be quite traumatic.

**You can help your child visualize the future** and anticipate the change by taking her with you to see her new home and environment as much as possible. Even you need that too. Remember that she is more bothered than you by the move, even though she doesn't have to worry about the material aspects as you do, and maybe even because of that. The move will remain more or less abstract to her and is by no means her choice.

**Let her participate as much as possible.**

Trust her with things to do as soon as possible. We tend to keep children away from the move with the idea of sparing our children the bother or quite simply to avoid having them under our feet. We are actually taking away something very important and constructive in their lives.

Practical help concerning the move to the new home eases the wrench of leaving the old one and helps acceptance of the change. Packing boxes and sorting things out are ways of getting to know the objects better and associating their presence with our own life. They provide a link between the old and the new, the past and the present. Children like to feel useful. Even a toddler can put all her fluffy toy animals in a box. An older child can seal boxes, name or number them, carry certain things…

Unless she's still a babe-in-arms, it's better for her to see what's going on and not be kept out of it all. It will give her the opportunity of strengthening her inner resources and experiencing the move from within, as well as helping her:

1) get over the loss of the old home,

2) gain awareness of herself and what remains the same beyond the change

3) imagine what her new life will be.

## Accompanying change of all sorts

### 1. Grieving the past

The stages of grieving are: denial, anger, negotiation, sadness and finally, acceptance. It's important to leave room (that means time and understanding) for all these emotions. Looking with the child at photos of the past, going over memories is a way of sharing the sweetness of nostalgia.

## 2. No-man's-land

Between two different worlds, two homes, two periods of life, it's helpful to allow oneself a no-man's-land, a mental space where it's possible to take temporary refuge and feel what is permanent. It's a way of bridging the gap between past and future, feeling the continuity between old and new. It's a place to look at the similarities and differences and imagine how the differences can be assets for times ahead.

This sort of interlude enables us to feel closer to ourselves, feel confidence in ourselves and in life. We can also look at the results of former changes and the positive things they brought.

## 3. Anticipation

Visualize the future. Imagine what will be. You can project yourself in the future and decide what you want to happen.

# 3
# The arrival of a new baby

Oh yes! It's a huge challenge, even an ordeal that some can't quite manage to get over. Mommy is less available and is busy looking after the baby. She's tired, maybe worn out by sleepless nights. The elder child must wait her turn to be looked after. She may even be told off because of the newcomer although she needs her mother as much as before. Sometimes she's supposed to make all the efforts just because the other is only a baby. What's more, she can have been promised a playmate and this one can't even catch a ball, just cry and sleep! Mommy kisses and cuddles him and he gets lots of presents. It's not fair!

The older the child the better she manages to cope with this irruption and disruption in her life. However, spacing out children has other inconveniences. It's not an ideal solution. Having brothers and sisters is an ordeal but getting over that is enriching.

Being the eldest is not easy, nor the youngest, without forgetting the one in the middle! In fact, no place is easy and even the word of reassurance "I love you just the same" doesn't help the situation.

In this book about emotions I don't go into relations between brothers and sisters, love and rivalry, imitation and conflicts. I just underline the importance of this change in a child's life.

She must renounce her position as the last-born, accept to share the parents' attention, sometimes her bedroom and toys as well. She has lost a privileged position and it has a huge impact on her. It's natural, normal and healthy that she should express **anger** because you've brought a new baby into the world. This arrival can make her feel threatened with separation. She may be worried, feel abandonned and even feel the **fear** of losing her parents' love, "Mommy wants another child, so that means I'm not enough for her!" Or, "I'm too old, she wants a baby and doesn't love me any more. "Or she may fear she's lost you for ever, "She's not coming back." This idea is very frequent, and seeing her mother come back from hospital (however well-informed she's been) is usually a great relief. Even though the child is somehow right, as it's true that her mother is not the same person she was before this new birth. And the mother has inevitably less time for her and she has to take second place, so she feels **sadness**.

By trying to avoid this distress, Cissie decided not to have a second child. But making the choice of having an only child is not a solution. Having to step down for a new baby is by no means easy but is interesting for future development. Are we to avoid the challenge or help our child accept it?

Trying to reason with children and moralizing are useless attitudes, and even hurtful ways of managing the situation. It's comforting to show her that you understand her difficulty, can listen to all her emotions and help her over the emotional hurdle towards acceptance.

Rather than making a list of all the advantages of having a brother or sister, why not get her to make his own list, without omitting the drawbacks?

This newcomer who disturbs the former pattern of life may be a step-father (-mother), or half-sister(s) or brother(s). Any new member of the family is disruptive of the previous order and thus plays havoc with emotions. Recomposed families are rarely easy. Your child has to accept new members but may not like them very much. You may have chosen a new partner but the children don't ever choose their brothers and sisters. It's possible to appreciate one another and get along well as long as things are said and everybody's emotions are respected.

# 4
# Parental disputes

Do you often quarrel with your partner? Is bitterness your predominant feeling? Do you think it's better not to say anything to your children to avoid upsetting them? Be careful! They're not stupid. They feel things even if you think you've been careful not to have a quarrel in their presence (especially so, as the tension of your avoidance is a warning that there's danger and all their senses are in alert mode). Even when they're asleep, part of them continues to capture what is going on. This conditions their dreams, nightmares and unconscious mental images. If they're not aware of where these come from, they're incapable of putting words to them and are far more disturbed. When you can identify things, it enables you to put them at a distance and make them less invasive.

Children suffer terribly from parental disputes, especially if they don't understand but just witness the surface events without knowing about the deeper causes. Listen to what they have to say before talking to them. Dare to touch on the problem and, even if you are exceedingly angry, be respectful of the parent you're criticizing, who is both your partner and their father or mother.

First of all, you need do no more than listen without judging or accusing, without justifying your position or excusing your partner but just being attentive to what the child has to say about her feelings. "How do you feel when I quarrel with Daddy?"

"I know it's not easy for you when Mommy and I are angry at one another. What do you feel in your heart?" (and breathe in deeply to be able to listen without reacting).

"I'm sure you're worried when you hear us quarrelling. What do you say to yourself?"

It's counter-productive to plead your cause. You're speaking to a child, not a judge, there's no need focus on one or other, but on what your child is feeling. She needs the opportunity to speak so she knows she's important, and it's crucial to hear out her thoughts and doubts.

It's important to answer her questions when they are really in connection with a need to know, not just fired at you to grab some element of truth. Be true to yourself and to her. Lies are emotionally disconnecting for everyone. Your have a right not to know things, be in doubt and to tell her so, but any pretence harms the connection.

Then she will need to be reassured. It's not her fault if her parents are not getting on well together. Whatever the situation you love her and always will.

# 5
## You're going to divorce

"I can't imagine myself calling them together, or even telling them one by one and looking them straight in the face to say, 'Daddy (Mommy) and I are going to divorce.'"

It's so difficult for so many parents to say what they feel and face their children's reactions and emotions that most of them prefer to say nothing until the day before or the very day of departure. Some even leave home without a word. The arguments are plentiful:

"I don't want them to suffer."

"If I tell them that I'm leaving and then I stay another week or month, they won't understand."

"It's no use hurting them earlier than necessary."

"It's no use talking to them until I'm certain of having found somewhere to live."

"I don't want them to see my hesitation."

"This is business between adults and it's no use bringing them into it."

Adults forget that they've usually taken time to think things over before making a decision. A separation involves a huge change in a child's life, so why shouldn't she be able to prepare it too?

"I'm waiting to make the decision", says Anne, the mother of three children. She doesn't want to alarm them for nothing.

Announcing changes of direction left, right and centre is obviously bad for children. But if you consider the time it took to make such a decision and get used to the idea of a separation, then announcing that decision only when you're sure means giving them very little time to assimilate things.

The sooner you speak to the children the better even telling them about the hesitations you have. Above all, listen to them. We are afraid of making them feel insecure with our own incertitudes but studies show that being suddenly faced with a the decision to divorce without having seen it coming is far more destabilizing than sharing the situation with the parents. Speak with your heart and your children will feel safe and understand that they are taken into account. You're keeping them informed and they'all accept that better than being subjected to a sudden and incomprehensible decision. Of course, there's suffering but it's pain that can be expressed and not something that has to be suffered in silence.

It's not to prevent the children from suffering that we say nothing but to avoid having to face their emotions and (im)pertinent reflections. We find it difficult to look our children in the eye and face their judgement. Rather than lying, it would be better to take heed of what their eyes tell us. We would thus avoid making many mistakes. There's very often a feeling of guilt towards the children behind this sort of hesitation. The belief that divorce deeply disturbs children is very tenacious. There's no doubt that it's preferable to all live together in one happy family. But when everything has been attempted to reconcile the couple, when love is no longer present, then separation frees everyone from an emotional stranglehold.

Many adults in psychotherapy tell of how they suffered from the dissension between their parents, their disputes, power games and the suffering they inflicted on themselves and each other. They feel anger that their parents didn't have the courage and honesty to separate and at having had to witness inacceptable words or acts. They feel anger at having inherited such a bad image of a couple, which has left a deep imprint and made their own relationships difficult.

The question is not to know whether divorce is destructive in itself but to ask: "How can we separate in an atmosphere of mutuel respect?" The impossibility of talking about it and expressing emotion, whether anger, sadness or fear is where the real harm lies.

## « Out of the mouth of babes and sucklings come grains of truth »

Children are well aware when their parents don't get along. They feel it without necessarily being able to name it. Even if the parents make sure to keep their disputes well away from childish ears they connect to the information at source.

Susan had been thinking of separating from her husband for some time but hadn't said anything to him. She swore to me that her children knew nothing, so I suggested she lend a more attentive ear to what they were saying. That very evening, to her amazement, her son of six asked her, "Mommy, if you divorce, who do I go with?"

Fortunately, we had prepared some answers together. She had been able to listen and, after the conversation, his performance in arithmetic improved. Susan immediately

257

understood that since her son had lots of unanswered questions his school-work had suffered, especially division! It's understandable that division becomes difficult when the family is likely to be divided.

Children feel things but daren't talk about them, being too afraid of breaking the secret, making things worse and even accelerating the separation. That doesn't mean they don't need to talk about it. It's up to the adults to take the first step.

## Is separation traumatic?

Except when there's violence directed at or around them or if they are being submitted to sexual abuse, children never want their parents to break up. Nonetheless, what children accuse their parents of is not the separation but the extent to which they were not informed, listened to or taken into account. The separation is necessarily painful but has no need to be toxic. Some children are very disturbed by a divorce but many are relieved when things are clarified. They will have two parents to talk with more easily than before when silence was the rule. They will soon feel freer, more light-hearted and better able to get on with their own lives.

When Sylvia's parents eventually separated she was seriously upset, although she was thirty. A lot of family taboos were lifted and secrets revealed. She realized she had lived all her childhood in a false situation and that everything she had intuitively felt about her parents' relationship was perfectly true! She had never been able to quite believe the façade they hid behind. She knew they weren't happy together, but she had never been able to lift the veil. Having had a deformed example of love and marriage, she experienced many setbacks and heartbreaks in her own life. Her parents' separation was painful but beneficial, enabling her to set herself free from the past and meet the man she is now living with. As a little girl she would never have wanted her parents to separate, yet she thinks that if her father had left earlier she would have found life a lot easier. She thought he was making her mother miserable and was angry at his behavior, all the while feeling angry with her mother for being so browbeaten and miserable. Her father used to flee the family, come home late and avoid going on holiday with his wife and daughter. Had she been able to see them separately, she would have been able to build a better relationship with each parent.

Paradoxically, a divorce may help children discover their father. Thanks to the visiting days, weekends and holidays, they sometimes see him more often, without him getting home late, sleeping at the weekends or bringing home work that's urgent. Unfortunately, some fathers disappear after a separation and lose contact with their children.

Our foremost duty to our children, after feeding and protecting them, is to be happy. If a divorce makes that more possible, then the children will welcome it. That doesn't mean that it's easy going. The necessary groundwork of getting over the loss and building new relationships with each parent is something to be worked on.

Separation is not traumatic in itself. It's the forbidden anger, fear, sadness, denial of emotions and the impossibility of expressing feelings that make a divorce traumatic. However, bringing up children alone, which falls to the lot of the mother for the most part, is certainly not easy. It would be beneficial for everybody if society made more provisions for isolated parents although the situation has changed for the better over the last decade.

## Your children want you to find happiness and fulfillment

We tend to imagine that our children think about and judge us as did our parents.

Patricia had been living alone for a long time with her children. She had never accepted another man in her life, thinking that her children (eight and ten) wouldn't stand her replacing their father. When she finally opened her ears to what they had to say, she found, to her surprise that they hoped she would have another love in her life.

Paula lived alone with her sixteen-year old son, not daring to go out in the evening because she was afraid of what he would think and was trying to compensate his father's abandon. In fact, he really wanted her to go out and enjoy herself but didn't dare say so for fear of her interpreting it as lack of love on his part. They used to squabble because they were both trying to protect the other although simultaneously feeling anger at the self-imposed imprisonment.

## Can an absent father be replaced?

There's a very high (too high) percentage of fathers who don't see their children after their divorce or separation. It's often to avoid facing the pain or their feeling of guilt that they wipe out the past. There are even agencies who help people to run away by having them reported as missing! Then they're given a new identity, usually in another country and disappear completely.

But what about the children?

All parents are responsible for themselves and the image they give to their children, not to mention messages they transmit, more by their behavior than by any words.

I don't think the mother should be the one to transmit the image of the father. Certain French psychoanalysts have made the mother entirely responsible for the father-image, going to the extent of saying that the actual absence of father is not important, the significant factor being the absence or presence of the paternal image in the mother's words and concept.

When the father isn't daily present, he is more easily idealized, whereas his presence at home would inevitably expose him to mundane problems to be resolved. Sandra confided, "My father was God to me!" and then came the little voice saying: "He was never there." Such words reveal the all-powerful image that had been attributed to him and the impact of his absence. Sandrine now finds it difficult to understand how such a saintly mother, who devoted herself to such a God-like father, could be so depressed, submissive and passive. Children don't need idealized parents but do need real people. Even if reality is not wonderful it will always be healthier for their development than some fictional version of life. Emotions will be better coped with when facts are faced.

## How to announce a separation

Of course, take your time to announce the news gently, talking of yourself and your feelings, and then being ready to listen to the children without worrying about you all crying together – as long as you don't count on them for consolation.

No use anticipating by answering questions that haven't been asked and maybe not even been thought about. They'll come in their own good time. This underlines the importance of talking early on.

There is no need to judge anybody nor justify yourself. Acknowledging what they perceive, feel, imagine and say will help them to through this difficult time. Their healthy feelings of anger, sadness and fear need to be aired and taken into account.

# 6
# Accidents, sickness and suffering

Although we are responsible for our health by our choice of lifestyle, food and our ability to manage our emotions and stress, we can't control everything. Nobody is accident-proof and sickness always comes as a surprise. We can't protect our children from pain and this is one of the most difficult things for a parent to face. Parents may ask their children to be brave, swallow their tears and hide their suffering so as not to put their parents through something so trying.

However, refusing to hear the pain and crying can be devastating and profoundly harm a child for life.

Sam is in his fifties and has been sent to hospital for acute peritonitis that he hadn't felt, although it had been gaining on him for weeks. Right from childhood he had learnt how not to feel anything.

A child can't imagine losing you and will do anything to help. Yes, even when she's driving you crazy, it's to protect you.

A child will express what she has been given the right to express, and can go to the extent of not feeling suffering if she sees it's more comfortable for you. She is capable of folding in on her pain or actually putting it aside and anesthetizing herself to avoid feeling anything.

It's maybe not best for the child to congratulate her on swallowing her tears. If a nurse asks her to be strong or says that the injection doesn't hurt, you're welcome to intervene and tell your child that she is the only one to know what she feels in her body and whether it hurts or not. She has the right to say so. In the same way if a visitor, whether family or not, says, "You're a big girl" You may reply, "She doesn't have to assume the difficulty you might have coping with your feelings. It's good to cry and complain if it hurts!"

If you listen and sympathize with her tears, your child will feel understood and helped and will find it that much easier to stand whatever pain she has to face.

If she's been sent to a hospital where you can't be with her, it's easy to explain that sometimes people don't know how to cope with suffering and that's why they praise the absence of any show of emotion, suggesting she should say, "I'm the one who's sick, it's my body and I'm the one that knows what hurts and what doesn't, and I have the right to feel pain and say so."

Do help your child to cry, tremble, whimper and even shout if she is in great pain in order to physiologically free herself from stress. She may be a bother to the doctors and nurses but she's so much more important!

# Chapter X

## Some Ideas For Living More Happily With Our Children

Beyond your role as a parent, you are a person, as is each child, and you both have needs. Conflicting needs between the two may create a form of competition, usually unconscious but very unhealthy.

The next few pages will expose some key ideas and valuable tools to help you avoid power games and be fully yourself.

# 1

# Be happy

Small children like to find routine in their daily life which gives them their bearings, but when routine means submitting unhappily to the daily grind, as the French say, **"métro, boulot, télé, dodo"** (metro, work, telly, sleep) children watch and wonder why. Does working at school and growing up necessarily involve alienation? We are our children's first models.

It's no good making sacrifices for them and your happiness is one of the most fundamental elements of their own fulfillment, because it encourages them to grow, freeing them of the responsibility of your happiness. A happy parent is that much more available and affectionate to his children.

It's true that the needs of the newborn are an absolute priority but beyond that stage any sacrifice poisons the relationship as you would inevitably begrudge it to the child, whether knowingly or unknowingly. Whatever the hardship consented and subsequent stress bravely born you will find it more and more difficult to give him what you truly want to give. Allowing time for resting, seeing friends, doing sport, going out and generally taking care of yourself is indispensable so as not to feel exasperated at the slightest hitch.

Sacrifice is mostly a woman's temptation but some men are ready to sacrifice their life for what they imagine their children's needs to be. Sacrifice is rarely 'for free' and parents inevitably (very likely unconsciously) expect something in return. Children will learn later that some idea of exchange was involved, that there was no true gift, with both the 'give' and the 'take' being decided by the adult without any negotiation between the two parties.

So as not to feel the frustration inherent to sacrifice, many women employ the technique of over-compensation. They forget their own needs and emotions and centre themselves only on their children. They mollycoddle their children, being over-protective, hyper-attentive and try to make themselves absolutely indispensable, ready to give everything, satisfy the slightest wish and automatically forbid the child to show any independence or anger. How could he need anything because his mother provides everything? However, the anger she's forbidding is her also own, for she has inevitably hoarded an immense unconscious anger which could well explode later or be turned against him.

It's so important to live your own life for yourself and not by proxy, via your children.

## Children try to repair their parents

If a parents are depressed, worried or unhappy and whether they show it or not, the child will feel it intuitively and try to help repair them.

Mary had always been a sweet child, without any problems. She always had a smile and some little joke to share. She was funny and would play all sorts of pranks, a real little clown. Apparently her childhood had been a happy one but in fact Mary had never felt the right to be herself.

Her mother was depressed and unhappy and since she never talked about it, Mary felt it must be *her* fault. Confusedly, she felt she was out of place and unwanted and tried to earn the right to exist by asking for as little as possible and making her mother laugh.

Mary controlled herself to exclude her needs and desires, hiding her feelings behind a permanent smile. Her self-imposed mission was to make her mother happy and she kept that smile all her life, whatever the circumstances. Always apparently carefree, she never seemed affected by anything. Always ready to help, she systematically put other people's needs before her own and her life was guided by convictions such as, "I don't have needs", "I don't have the right to have my own life" and "Children are a burden".

Naturally, Mary worked professionally in a humanitarian organization, giving to others. She found it difficult to keep a steady relationship with a partner and, at forty-eight, had no children.

How can we possibly imagine sparing our children by hiding our problems? Children know, so the best thing is to talk openly. If her mother had been able to speak about the reasons why she was sad Mary would not have felt guilty and bound to repair. She wouldn't have thrown herself into the dangerous and impossible mission of trying to heal her mother. She would have felt the right to have and satisfy her own needs.

Until Françoise Dolto spoke up, it was generally thought that children shouldn't be told about their parents' problems, so as not to worry them, as they were too young to understand grownup affairs. And what is more, it wasn't any of their business! Today, we know that children can understand things very well if time is taken to explain.

Talking to them is reassuring because it enables them to put words to impressions. It helps children feel they are individuals with separate identities who don't have to help or heal their parents or burden themselves with their problems...

We must remember that all the problems we refuse to face will be taken on by our children and grandchildren. Is that what we really want?

Excessive shyness, lack of self-confidence, feelings of shame, guilt or anxiety, marital problems, professional setbacks are not genetically programmed and yet they're transmitted from generation to generation.

How do you feel in your couple, your job, your life? These questions shouldn't be buried or your children are likely to have to struggle with them.

If you meet a difficult moment financially speaking, are out of work, have your job threatened or are having heated arguments with your boss, you can talk about it. Without alarming them, you can share your feelings and worries so that your children won't bear the burden alone and unknowingly.

Secrets are always toxic. So, your child doesn't have a father? You were raped when you were seventeen? You've gone bankrupt? You've been to prison? You never managed to pass an exam? Your father used to hit you? These are things your children can be told hear! Tell them also what has been happy in your life but without avoiding the difficult patches. If you don't talk about the dark parts, they may leave indelible traces. You could one day be amazed to learn that they have been in the same ruts, been raped at the same age (or met someone who has, or even committed the act), have gone bankrupt, been to court (and maybe prison) failed in their studies, mismanaged things or got beaten up.

The process of repetition is a means of finding and feeling something that happened to you, of being able to understand yourself and find a better way out of the same dilemma. You can free them of the weight of your past just by expressing your experiences and feelings.

And don't forget the joy you have inside. Breathe in and feel the simple pleasure of being. Beware of letting yourself get weighed down by the day-to-day humdrumness of life and its problems. Take the time to feel the love that you have for others around, know that you are progressing along your own path through life and are pleased with it.

# 2

# Tune in and listen

*"O.K., I'm ready to listen, but he won't say anything!"*

I've heard this heartfelt complaint so many times from desperate and disillusioned parents. It's not enough to feel open and welcoming to make a child to speak out. He needs the assurance that he will be listened to without any judgment whatsoever concerning what he feels. Let's face it, it's sometimes difficult to simply listen to a problem without taking sides, suggesting opinions or solutions, accepting the emotions without trying to reassure or patch up.

All efforts at contributing orders, threats, sermons, lessons, advice, humiliation or blame, not to mention flattery, excessive reassurance or diversions, must be out of the question. The child will understand that his emotions aren't welcome and that you are trying to minimize them or think he cannot sort things out for himself.

Each time we solve a problem for him, we're taking away a possibility of developing his independence. Each time we explain something he already knows, we're humiliating him and making him feel small.

Listening involves tuning into the emotion so that the child feels accepted the way he is and feels himself to be. It's not so much a question of listening to what he says as echoing the core feeling. If he tells you about a dispute with a friend, teacher, brother or father, he's probably telling you about a failure or anticipating a problem. It's a question of emotions to be listened to rather than the hard facts! Tune into his feelings by listening with your body and with your heart. Sometimes he won't use the language of words but the language of play and make-belive.

The way people hold themselves is a sure guide to what they are feeling. By putting yourself into the same posture as your child, you are making yourself available to him and will hear him that much better. Try it out. Slump back in your chair with your legs apart and your arms swinging, and you'll realize you are quite unable to feel fear. Certain positions make emotions quite impossible and your body sends subliminal messages to your child. How can he trust you to be in empathy with his uncomfortable feelings if you're comfortably sitting back in your armchair while he's confiding his shyness with a girlfriend? It's a position that makes it physiologically impossible to be in contact with his feelings. He will inwardly know that you're not really listening, just following the words but not his vital experience.

## Listen with your heart

Dare to let his feelings resonate in you. But that doesn't mean being contaminated by them.

It's not worth you crying as well! Your child needs your compassion and to know that you know what he feels, that you understand what he's going through, not with your mind but with your heart, but he doesn't want or need to drag you down with him. Even worse, if you start crying he's likely to interrupt what he's confiding to spare you pain and tears!

It's better not to mix the bitter leftovers from your own childhood with what your child is telling you. If you have a whole pack of unexpressed or repressed feelings, they could very well make a tangle of emotional knots that's difficult to undo. So, be careful to identify and put aside your feelings, which should be sorted out later but as soon as possible.

A helpful idea to maintain the right presence is to breathe in deeply through your nose and imagine you're taking air into your abdomen, right down to the base of your spine.

Solving the problem is not your job but helping him express what he feels and accepting his emotions as they flow most certainly is. Just send him love in exchange with neither fear, nor anger, nor sadness, in order to help him find the strength and confidence he needs to face his difficulty.


## The words you can use

You may want to help him describe his experience in the following terms:

—*It's hard for you to...*

—*It's difficult...*

—*I can see that... (you're sad, things haven't been easy for you today...).*

—*I imagine that...*

—*I understand that... makes you suffer.*

—*You're feeling sad at the idea of... (not seeing your house any more).*

—*You want to...(get your own back, never see him gain, call up...).*

—*You love...(music, birds, animals...).*

## To help him go even further, ask open questions.

Questioning with *why* may make him feel guilty and seeks thoughts not the inner feelings. If you try out *what* and *how* you'll see the difference:

—*What's going on?*

—*What does that make you feel like?*

—*What do you feel when…?*

—*What did you feel when…?*

—*What did you think when…?*

—*What makes you saddest, angriest, (according to the emotion displayed), etc?*

—*What do you miss most?*

—*What's bothering you the most?*

—*What do you think about (someone's attitude, behavior…)?*

—*How do you feel about… (happy or unhappy event)?*

—*How do you see the situation?*

—*What makes you afraid?*

—*What makes you most afraid?*

—*What do you need?*

# 3

## se your body, heart and mind to communicate person-to-person

### Kisses and cuddles

Massages, fighting, tickling, catching one another are all irreplaceable means of saying "I love you", "I like you just the way you are" and helping the child build up a solid feeling of confidence in his body and his being, as long as the limits he indicates are respected and you stop as soon as he tells you to.

It's very tempting to tickle a baby and and smother him with kisses but do we do it for our pleasure or for his good? If his pleasure matches ours, that's fine but otherwise it's time to stop. An adult hasn't the right to use a child's body for his own pleasure and all children must know that their body belongs to them and that their limits must be respected.

### Dream together

If your daughter drools over a gorgeous wedding dress in a shop window, it's not the moment to bring her down to earth, so join in her dream, imagining, "I'd want flowers in my hair and it would be a sunny day with lots of people, and you could wear that dress and we'd eat those yummy cakes."

If your small son comes to a standstill in front of an electric car, he'll enjoy you dreaming along with him, "You love driving, don't you! I can just see you driving round the garden, *vroum, vroum!* That would really be fun."

## Talk about your feelings

It's connecting and constructive to talk about what's going on in your daily life. Did something unfair or distressing happen at work? Were you frustrated after a call from your mother-in-law? Are you upset and angry about the death of a friend who should have been too young to die? Is there some jealousy with a colleague? When you share your feelings with them, your children feel close to you and reassured about their importance in your life? That's the best way to present fundamental models for them to use in their own lives when they have to cope with awkward moments.

## Recall your life

It's a way of sharing who you are as a person, not to make them feel guilty with comments such as "When I was young, we didn't have all you have but we were fine" but to let them get to know you better, understand you better and find their roots. They will enjoy hearing about facts, anecdotes, events and reactions concerning everyone but also about what *you* thought and felt and talked about – they're all precious links.

## Talk about everything

Children are more intelligent than we give them credit for and can surprise us with the pertinence and wisdom of their ideas. Yet we keep so much back from them, thinking that they're too young.

Thanks to television children are so much better informed than we were, so it's easier for us to bring up and explore all sorts of subjects to enable them to avoid superficial or misleading interpretations. It's surprising to find out how worldly-wise they can be.


## Communicate soul to soul

We mustn't forget that our children are not only our children. They are humans, with their own being and destiny. We meet with them in this life, we even have a mission towards them and a necessary role but they are individuals who will make their own choices.

*Your children are not your children.*
  *They are the sons and daughters*
  *of Life's longing for itself.*
  *They come through you but not from you,*
  *And though they are with you yet they belong not to you.*

*—Khalil Gibran,* The Prophet

# 4
# Feel how good it is to be a parent

It's so nice to surround yourself with photos and drawings to underline your love for them, to awaken your tenderness when they stain the sofa, refuse to clear the table or get bad marks at school.

Taken up with daily chores we sometimes forget that we're happy living together. All parents agree on one thing: childhood goes past far too quickly. So let's not miss those precious moments!

There'll be time enough to make the house spick and span when they've left and it seems empty without their noise and laughter...

# Conclusion

Emotions are not dangerous. They are not only the salt of life but it's very essence. Each time you silence your or your child's heart, doubt your inner voice or fail to listen to what your child is trying to tell you, you are limiting your life and his. It's the way we accept and act on our and their emotions that is the key issue.

"The end is in the means", said Mahatma Gandhi. Let's listen to our children so they'll know how to listen, respect them so they, in turn, will respect others and accept to feel and free their own emotions. Then we'll cease projecting our own suffering and be able to accept their tears. Let's accompany them on their path through life according to the stages of their growth, help them express what they are, find their identity and trust their capabilities, desires and needs. It's quite simple a question of encouraging them to feel, name and live their emotions to the fullest.

Spending time on emotions is something very new. We're doing pioneering work so it's all right if we don't always quite manage to do it as well as we would wish. Sometimes we're bound to trip up but at least we're on the right road.

Happy travelling!

1 Françoise Dolto, Les chemins de l'education, Gallimard 1994 as yet untranslated ito English ( Literal translation: Educational pathways). She was an extremely well-known French pediatrician who had immense impact via books and radio on intelligent parental guidance, always reasoning from the child's point of view.

2 Founder of the "Aware Parenting Institute" in the USA, she has written many books over the past 20 years;

3 An American author, Dr Harold Bessell has written many books on parenting and human development.

4 Alice Miller (1923-2010) was a world-renowned psychotherapist of Polish origin who wrote a great number of books (widely translated) on the abuse of children by their parents. She had a critical viewpoint on Freudian psychoanalysis after having practised for over 20 years.

5 A communication dilemma formalized by Gregory Bateson (Palo Alto School – Mental Research Institute) when conflicting messages are received. One message negates the other, leading to mutually invalidating responses. It is logically impossible to opt out of the situation because of the inherent contradiction.

6 This is an image coined by Alain Crespelle, who was my first psychotherapist and my model for years. He died in 1999 and I pay him hommage by using these words, which so clearly show the reflection of our emotions on our children's behavior.

7 I like Catherine Dolto-Tollich's very expressive formula where sweet words are nice to receive and quite different from 'stone words' which are hard and hurtful.

8 Other potential factors include: sugar, conservatives, colorants... or a food intolerance.

45859016R00158

Made in the USA
Middletown, DE
15 July 2017